"SHUT UP!" HE EXPLAINED

By June and William Noble

Steal This Plot, Middlebury, Vermont, 1985.
The Psychiatric Fix, New York, 1981.
The Private Me, New York, 1980.
How To Live With Other People's Children, New York, 1978.
The Custody Trap, New York, 1975.

"Shut Up!" He Explained

A Writer's Guide to the Uses and Misuses of Dialogue

by William Noble

Paul S. Eriksson

PUBLISHER

MIDDLEBURY, VT. 05753

For Junie

Manufactured in the United States of America

10 9 8 7 6 5 4 3 2 1

Library of Congress Cataloging-in-Publication Data

Noble, William.
  "Shut Up!" He Explained

  Bibliography: p.
  Includes index.
  1. Authorship. 2. Dialogue. I. Title.
PN218.N63   1987   808'.02   87-20053
ISBN 0-8397-7777-9

Contents

"SHUT UP!" HE EXPLAINED

Preface

Dialogue is...

A friend called one day. "Someone I've known for thirty years sent me a manuscript," he said. "A fascinating story. You'll love the plot."

"A published writer?" I asked.

"She sets the story in Charleston, South Carolina, at the turn of the century—the old South embracing the Industrial Revolution, black-white love interests...." My friend paused. "She's always wanted to write."

Unpublished, I thought. "You want me to look it over."

"I know you're busy."

"Did you enjoy reading it?"

"She's a social worker—she understands people."

"You think it might go?"

"I'd really appreciate your thoughts...."

The manuscript arrived two days later, neatly bundled, with the barest note from my friend. Three hundred and forty typewritten pages, centered properly; a prefatory statement and a brief background on the author. I began reading.

And by page fifteen I knew the manuscript had no hope. The storyline was interesting, the characters richly endowed, the historical perspective clear and accurate.

What happened?

This happened: on page four the young hero's superior says to him,

> "Talk to Harrison, show him what's here, then call me."
>
> "Yes sir."
>
> "You know *what's* here?"
>
> "Yes sir, I think so."
>
> "Are you sure?"
>
> "Yes sir."

On page six:

> "Good morning, Mr. Harrison."
>
> "Good morning."
>
> "Would you like to see some samples?"
>
> "Yes."
>
> "They are over here, sir."
>
> "Oh, they are, are they?"
>
> "Yes sir."

On page fifteen:

> "Is Harrison here?"
>
> "Yes sir."
>
> "Good morning, Mr. Harrison, have you seen the samples?"
>
> "Your young man has been showing them to me—what's your name again, son..."

And so forth.

Dialogue. This is what tripped the author and turned what could have been an interesting story into one that barely plods. *Dialogue must move a story*, Peggy Simpson Curry wrote more than 20 years ago, and when it doesn't, everything—storyline, character development, mood enhancement—grinds to a halt.

Let's be clear about one thing, though: dialogue is one of the most difficult skills for any writer to master. The sense of reality to be conveyed is often misunderstood because we're dealing with an essential sleight-of-hand. What is, is often not enough, just as what passes as fact is not the same as truth. Dialogue must not only be factual, it must be *dramatically* factual, and in this way the writer must convey not so much what is said as the sense of reality, spiced dramatically.

In the passages of dialogue by the social worker-author, we can't deny the evident conscientiousness. She has faithfully recorded each conversation.

The reader's reaction is—so what?

The writer will probably respond:

- That's the way people talk.
- Those are his exact words.
- That's the way it happened.

Maybe, but it doesn't make a story. Here's Samuel Johnson, more than two hundred years ago:

Tom Birch is as brisk as a bee in conversation, but no sooner does he take a pen in hand, than it becomes a torpedo to him, and benumbs all his faculties.

Conversation, then, is not dialogue. And when we insert conversation on the written page assuming it is good, realistic dialogue, it's like throwing cold water on whatever drama we are building. Conversation is...conversation; dialogue is dialogue. They are easy to mix up and hard to separate.

But the diligent writer perseveres. He or she *knows* what will crackle on the written page, and what will die.

"Where do you live?"

"230 State Street."

That's conversation.

"You live around here?"

"If you want to call it living."

That's dialogue.

In some respects good dialogue-writing is a mirage. It *seems* to be realistic, it seems to portray actual people doing actual things.

But it doesn't. Not really.

Here's Geoffrey Bocca from his book, *You Can Write a Novel:*

Of all aspects of novel writing, none plays a greater con

job on the reader than dialogue. The art of dialogue lies in leading the reader to think that the characters are speaking as they do in everyday life, when they are doing nothing of the sort. What people speak in normal life is conversation, not dialogue. Conversation is exchange of information: 'What's the time?' 'Six o'clock'. That's conversation, but it is not dialogue.

Then what is dialogue? Perhaps the answer is more elusive than we might think. We can say what it is *not*, and that might be a good deal easier than artificial rules to define what it is. But we do know certain things: we recognize good dialogue when we read it, we're grabbed and shaken by its veracity. Is there any doubt that the following passage from John O'Hara's *Ten North Frederick* sparkles as dialogue?

"What do you think I've had you in my office for? To talk about baseball?"

"No sir."

"Then answer my question."

"*Which* question, sir? Gosh, you ask me a thousand questions, and I don't know which I'm supposed to answer."

"There's only one question. Are you guilty of smoking cigarettes in the toilet and endangering the property, the lives and property of this school?"

"I smoked. You know that, sir. I was caught."

Perhaps like a beautiful woman or a mystical experience, good dialogue is easier to recognize than it is to define. But there are certain guides we can follow: good dialogue will do each of the following:
- characterize the speaker;
- establish the setting;
- build conflict;
- foreshadow;
- explain.

For example, suppose we want to show a character's cynical

nature. A physical description will hardly do it, and if we call the person cynical, it certainly loses something in dramatic effect. So we put words in the character's mouth:

"Life's a bitch, man."

or

"I never trust a man who parts his name to the left. He's hiding something."

Here's John O'Hara again. A judge and lawyer are talking informally, and the judge suggests that a recently widowed female friend hire a young, bright, fresh lawyer, set him up in practice, and use him as a stud. The judge continues:

"...I'm telling you, it's a fair bargain. All she does is support him till he gets established. Why is it so much worse for a young guy to sleep with an elderly woman than a young girl to go to bed with an elderly man? You look around this club. You know yourself, half the members of this club are giving money to young girls for some kind of satisfaction."

"Half? That's pretty high."

"Arthur, your own friends are doing it, and you know it."

"No, I *don't* know it," said McHenry. "I suppose there are two or three..."

Now there's a cynical man, and O'Hara paints him through the use of his own words. The essence of his cynicism is furthered by the contrast with the other speaker who is certainly more forgiving. The two sides of the equation demonstrate character traits in both men, and we get to know them each a little better.

Dialogue in a vacuum, however, serves little purpose. A character saying something for no reason or without adding to the story wastes the reader's time and patience. It's like inserting an unwanted ingredient into a carefully orchestrated meal—it can have the effect of contaminating everything. Anthony Trollope said that dialogue must contribute to the telling of the story and that when extraneous matter is added the reader feels cheated. Arturo Vivante agrees. "There should be a nexus, link or connection between one line and another. The dialogue should make a point. The gist of it, its purport, should come through."

Suppose two characters are discussing a matter of importance, and in the course of their discussion they become increasingly agitated with one another. The tension between them is palpable. At this point the author has a choice: the verbal tension can result in physical action—one could strike the other, or simply walk away in disgust. Or the verbal parrying could be diffused by words that neutralize the conflict quickly. In each case, though, the author has to be on top of the characters' reactions. Nothing should interfere to misdirect the reader's attention. Otherwise the effect of the scene is lost, and so are the significance of the disagreement and its aftermath. For example, if the author interrupts the dialogue with a descriptive passage about the weather or about some third party not involved in the scene, or if the dialogue has little relation to what the characters are speaking about, the reader will just be confused. Trollope would ask: does it contribute to the telling of the story?

Characters greet each other and say good-bye in all phases of literature. They ask questions of and learn about one another repeatedly. *But they don't do it the way it's done in real life!*

"Hello Bob."

"Hi Jane."

"When were you born?"

"What's your address?"

"How old are you?"

"What kind of work do you do?"

"Good-bye, Bob."

"'Bye, Jane."

Real life is questions and comments like these. Good written dialogue ignores such phrases. Comings and goings don't need to be marked so assiduously; they can be implied by a descriptive passage indicating that so-and-so came in or left. In addition, one character might begin a statement with a declarative sentence:

"Glad you could make it..."

or

"I'll stop at Harry's on my way home..."

Arturo Vivante calls questions such as "when were you born?" and "how old are you?" irrelevant and pointless. In his mind they are *passport questions*, the type of drama-free interrogation we go through when we apply for a passport. Sure, they identify us, and if the reader would sit still for a word-report on who we are, a clear picture would emerge. The problem is... passport questions are just a report, they are not dramatic (unless the scene itself is dramatic, such as in a courtroom or a police interrogation), they don't make a story. Take age, for example. The only time it is important in dialogue is when it contributes to the telling of the story. If one of the characters lies about his/her age, then we have the tip of a curtain raised on characterization as well as on plot line. The story will move forward because the reader knows something at least one of the characters doesn't know. And perhaps the misstated age will affect the actions of other characters. Thus the plot is influenced. Otherwise, age and similar passport questions are best left to descriptive passages where they can be disposed of with a broader sweep.

What about this passage of dialogue?

"T-t-t-thank you, Henry."

"Aaaargh..." He sputtered, downing the milk.

"Um... you-ah-still t-t-think we... um... should do it... um... t-t-the people downstairs... um... aren't so sure."

"Aaaargh..."

"T-t-t-that milk doesn't look fresh."

In real life we all hem and haw, sometimes uncertain how to phrase words or uncertain even whether they should be said.

And I don't think there's anyone who hasn't sputtered when drinking something that went down the wrong way. Nor do I believe that at some point in our lives each of us hasn't stuttered out of embarrassment, nervousness, or simple uncertainty.

But do these things add to the telling of the story? The question is a key one. Are these mannerisms helpful in pushing the drama along? There's no doubt that such things occur in real life—we've all been exposed to them. Yet they have a tendency to distract the reader, to deflect attention from the unfolding story.

It's really the same distinction we made between conversation and dialogue. One is fact, the other is art. We can draw characters with life-like mannerisms, and we've achieved a realistic portrait. But what does it do to the drama of our story?

It slows it down and neutralizes it.

Then we have a story going nowhere.

This doesn't mean, however, that we can't have characters who will sputter or stutter or hem and haw, but the key is that we needn't portray these things incessantly. A stutterer, especially if this characteristic is important to how the story unfolds, can show this affliction once, twice at the outset and then rarely again. Respect the reader's ability to chronicle such a trait and to fit into a mental image of the character. A character who sputters can be presumed to act this way whenever the stimulus that brought on the initial sputtering reappears. It isn't necessary to show it repeatedly, even if such a trait does add to the telling of the story.

Let's examine sputtering a bit. When might it occur? Perhaps from indignation or pomposity or overindulgence...it's a mannerism that indicates dissatisfaction and explosive release. Now, we might describe a character sputtering, as in: "I can't believe it!" he sputtered..., but to attempt a word description of the sound, such as *aaargh*, and to write it repeatedly to define a character's reaction is a bit much. Use the character's own words to portray the sputtering, not the sounds he/she makes.

Even though we've all heard the real-life noise.

But sometimes we put our words on the written page, we follow all the rules, and it still isn't right. We know what we want our characters to say, we think we have them saying those things and in the way we'd like them said, but it just doesn't flow. We restudy what we've written, we even walk away and focus on something else, thinking this might break the pattern.

Even that doesn't work. What, then, can we do?

Here's John Sayles: "I always read my dialogue out loud, give it what actors call a 'cold reading' without dramatics or a great deal of inflection. Typewritten words have a lot of power—they look very official and convincing even though you know you just made them up. Your ear may catch what your eye is fooled by."

Consider this:

"I don't want to go, you can't make me go, no one can make me go."

"The problem isn't you, it's me. I'm the problem, just me. I want you to go, I really do."

On the written page it reads as two people in an intense disagreement. Clearly they are at an emotional pitch. But read it aloud, give the words no inflection...and we see it is overwritten. The repetitiveness doesn't add to the high level of the emotions, it makes the exchange melodramatic. Would this read better?

"I don't want to go, you can't make me," she said.

"The problem isn't you, it's me." His voice was tired.

A cold reading means a tight reading, it means dialogue that has no fat and fully contributes to the telling of the story. Try it.

But remember...no inflections, no drama. Avoid characterizing anything, even though the urge may be overpowering.

Perhaps the most important aim of dialogue writing is to fashion every speech so it doesn't bring the story to a dead stop. When we have characters meeting one another and the dialogue appears this way:

"How are you, Bob?"

"I'm fine, thank you. How are you?"

"I'm fine."

"Good!"

the story hasn't moved a bit. As we've seen, such exchanges may mirror real life, but they really have no place in fiction. Now suppose we carry the exchange a bit further to where the characters are seated comfortably:

"Did you notice the Wedgewood plate hanging in Sarah's house?"

"No, I didn't."

"I would have thought you'd seen it."

"I never looked at it."

"Why didn't you look at it?"

"Because I didn't."

"If you had looked, you might have seen something."

"Such as?"

"Whether Sarah had moved it the past 24 hours."

"Is that important?"

"Yes, it's important..."

This dialogue isn't bad, really, it's just dull. Questions and answers, each passage responding directly to the one immediately preceding. A symmetry that could lull us to sleep.

Most good dialogue, however, doesn't work this way. The questions and answers don't follow one another; in fact, some questions are never answered, and in any event good dialogue passages are not simple declarations or tidy examinations. They are what generally goes on between people when they're talking: uneven, sometimes unresponsive, often unprepared comments that provide a glimpse into the character of each speaker and into the relationship between the speakers. Good dialogue evokes drama, even though what the characters say may not be in neat order with each passage directly responsive to the one preceding it.

"This ship barely answers her helm."

"Maybe we better think about pumping the forward tanks."

The second passage is not directly responsive to the first. Yet the story does move forward.

Compare this:

"This ship barely answers her helm."

"Yeah, I know what you mean."

Ford Madox Ford, a prolific writer and contemporary of Hemingway, Fitzgerald, and Conrad, puts the approach to responsive dialogue in perspective: "One unalterable rule we had," he writes, "for the rendering of conversations, for genuine conversations that are an exchange of thought, not interrogatories or statements of fact—was that no speech of one character could ever answer the speech that goes before it. This is almost invariably the case in real life where few people listen, because they are always preparing their own next speeches..."

We'll see in the succeeding chapters how authors through the ages have utilized the technique Ford Madox Ford describes. But here's a sampling:

Ernest Hemingway in *A Farewell to Arms*:

"Tell me," he said, "what is happening at the front?"

"I would not know about the front."

"I saw you come down the wall. You came off the train."

"There is a big retreat."

"I read the papers. What happens? Is it over?"

"I don't think so..."

F. Scott Fitzgerald in *The Beautiful and Damned*:

"When we have a baby," she began one day—this, had already been decided, was to be after three years—"I want it to look like you."

"Except its legs," he insinuated slyly.

"Oh, except his legs. He's got to have my legs. But the rest of him can be you."

"My nose?"

Gloria hesitated...

Joseph Conrad in *The Rescue*:

"How unnaturally quiet! It is like a desert of land and water without a living soul."

"One man at least dwells in it," said d'Alcacer, lightly, "and if he is to be believed there are other men, full of evil intentions."

"Do you think it is true?" Mrs. Travers asked.

Before answering d'Alcacer tried to see the expression on her face but the obscurity was too profound already.

"How can one see a dark truth on such a dark night?" he said, evasively. "But it is easy to believe in evil, here or anywhere else . . ."

Dialogue writing is dramatic writing, and the techniques are there for us to follow. More than sixty years ago—about the time Ford Madox Ford was describing his approach to dialogue-writing—an obscure teacher of English set forth some ideas which expanded Ford's concept. Glenn Clark, the teacher, listed techniques any writer of fiction could—and should—follow:

1. Make your speeches short. No one in real life talks in long sentences, and no one except on platforms makes ten-minute speeches.

2. Do not hesitate to have one speaker break in on another. Interruptions and rapidity in 'taking one's cues' keep the dialogue lively.

3. Instead of answering a question, have the character addressed ask another.

4. Instead of a character answering a question with a statement of what was done, have him tell why it was done.

5. Have a character ignore the question and anticipate the next and answer that instead.

6. Have a different character answer a question by using different words from the questioner.

Put it together, what do we have? One simple rule, really. Trollope's dictum: *dialogue should contribute to the telling of the story*! How it's done and the specific instances in which it is done are what we'll explore in the chapters to come.

Part A

The Master Keys to Dialogue

Prelude

The opportunities for the use of dialogue in fiction and non-fiction as infinite as whatever the imagination can conjure. Yet certain circumstances stand out. Dialogue appears in some situations more frequently than others, and it has more influence, more impact on storyline in these contexts. Dialogue use—or misuse—is crucial here to the effectiveness of the story, and if it's not done well, we won't be happy with the result.

Think of dialogue as occurring in situations. Dialogue is part of the overall structure, no more important than character or plot development, but no less so. We want to use dialogue, and we know that it should serve some useful purpose. It must *do* something! It must perform.

The essential question is. . .how do we do it? The answer is in understanding the situations in which we want our dialogue to appear. I don't mean the fact situations in our story, such as the bedroom scene, the car chase, the torture scene. I mean the purpose we want our dialogue to perform. Once we come up with the scene and decide there should be dialogue in it, then we face the basic question of which dialogue situation or situations we want to portray.

And specifically we'll fall back on those that are most substantial and most common.

I call these the Master Keys to Dialogue because they have the power to unlock the creative mysteries in all of us. They provide us with the power to master the many dialogue situations.

There are only six Master Key situations, and they are crucial for developing a believable storyline. They have been used by writers through the ages, and their importance lies not so much in their frequency of use as in their pervasive influence over the way a story proceeds.

Can we imagine, for example, not using dialogue to show or develop character? Can we write about people and put words in their mouths without, at the same time, being fully aware of what the words might show about them? Do we, in real life, turn off our antennae when we are speaking with another; do we simply block out an awareness of motivation or effect?

Not unless we expect to live in a robot-filled world.

The Master Key situations should be well handled in order for good, believable dialogue to ensue. It matters little that narrative portions of the work ring with truth and clarity or that descriptive passages evoke mind-tingling images or even that the style is unique and eye catching. If the dialogue doesn't work, the result will be no different than when a work of art is defaced. People look forward to reading dialogue. Some even skip narrative passages in order to feast on the dialogue, and when it doesn't measure up, the feast soon turns to tasteless fare.

Become familiar with these Master Keys. Use them to generate the story and be happy that they work for us.

Because they *do* work.

1

Suppose We Want to Create Tension

What do these situations have in common?

- A man and woman are walking hand in hand. The man is in love with the woman and wants to tell her so. There is no way of knowing how the woman will respond.
- It is a hot, tropic evening and a man and woman have just finished making love. They are close together on the bed, their attention on one another. A black widow spider crawls under the sheets.
- A woman has been abducted, but she has fought off her kidnappers. She finds herself alone, on a dirt road, in an unknown place with the temperature dropping. She has had little experience with the outdoors.

As storylines, the three situations tend to catch the eye. There is uncertainty and mystery and danger. The characters are not plodding along in relative tranquility. Something is troubling them. Matters are not under absolute control.

Tension is the answer. Each of the storylines has tension or conflict built into the circumstances. Tension is the basic molder of a story; it's what catches the reader's eye and holds the reader's attention. Tension is the key that turns dull material into something we all want to read.

Tension is appropriately portrayed through dialogue; in fact, dialogue without tension has little going for it. Consider the following two exchanges:

"I think we should walk to the restaurant," he said.
"I-I don't know," she responded.

- - -

"I think we should walk to the restaurant," he said.
"Sure," she responded.

It's the woman's answer that determines the level of tension. In the first example, her uncertainty projects to the reader. Why is she uncertain, what's she afraid of? In the second example, she's agreeing but there's no drama in it. Hence, no tension. It's like a report. There's no mystery here, no unanswered questions.

Dialogue must create tension to be effective, and there are a variety of ways this can be done. The first and most obvious, of course, is by argument or disagreement. Two or more people not seeing eye to eye. This doesn't need to be a screaming match, nor a basic "yes-no" standoff. The disagreement can be portrayed subtly yet distinctly. In *The Cider House Rules*, John Irving has his protagonist Homer Wells in conversation with Candy Kendall alongside the conveyor belt at the packing house. They are talking about Candy's pregnancy, which Homer was responsible for:

"If I work as hard as I can, Candy told him, "it's possible that I'll miscarry."

It was not possible, Homer Wells knew.

"What if I don't want you to miscarry?" Homer asked her.

"What if?" Candy asked.

"What if I want you to marry me, and to have the baby?" Homer asked.

They stood at one end of the conveyor belt in the packing house; Candy was at the head of the line of women who sized and sorted the apples—who either packaged them or banished them to cider. Candy was retching even though she had chosen the head of the line because that put her nearest the open door.

"We have to wait and see," Candy said between retches.

"We don't have long to wait," said Homer Wells. "We don't have long to see"...

What Irving is doing is using questions and declarative statements. "What if...?" is really another way of saying "I don't..." and by doing this he is developing the disagreement between Candy and Homer. The subtlety of the disagreement is apparent in the fact that neither Homer nor Candy provides a direct, stiff resounding "No!" to the other's suggestions. yet is there any doubt about who feels which way?

And by having Candy retch during the conversation, Irving is underlining her feelings about having the baby and about the immediacy of having to make a decision. These uncertainties, coupled with the disagreement, are what build tension into this exchange.

Sometimes, however, disagreement can rise beyond the subtleties and become blatant anger. This disagreement has escalated into sheer fury. Though examples in literature abound, suppose we look at one by a writer whose masterful portrayals have entertained us through the centuries. In William Shakespeare's *Romeo and Juliet* we have Juliet's father, Capulet, just informed that Juliet will not marry Paris, the suitor her father has chosen. The tension in the scene is evident from the intensity of Capulet's wrath:

Capulet: ...But fettle your fine joints against Thursday next, go with Paris to Saint Peter's Church, or I will drag thee on a hurdle thither. Out, you green-sickness carrion! Out, you baggage! You tallow face!

Lady Capulet: Fie, fie! What, are you mad!

Juliet: Good father, I beseech you on my knees,
              hear me with patience but to speak a
              word.

Capulet: Hang thee, young baggage! disobedient
              wretch! I tell thee what: get thee to church
              o' Thursday, or never after look me in the
              face; speak not, reply not, do not answer
              me; my fingers itch. Wife, we scarce
              thought us blest that God had lent us but
              this only child; but now I see this one is
              one too much, and that we have a curse in
              having her. Out on her hilding!

Note how Capulet exhibits his fury: name calling, threats, disgust, even a refusal to listen. The anger is not on both sides—only from Capulet, yet tension is certainly created. A disagreement does not have to show anger reflected from each of the parties. It's enough if one of them is angry and the anger is sharp and loud. The fact that others in the scene try to calm Capulet, even appease him, does not limit the tension. It is the anger, itself, which creates the tension.

Sometimes, it isn't even necessary to produce give-and-take dialogue when there is anger. An appropriate monologue can do the trick, the words themselves conveying the depth of feeling by virtue of the subject matter. Suppose we have a young man at his father's graveside, swearing vengeance on those he believes killed his father? Or suppose we have a young woman who has suffered much and who yearns for the release of death? Her solitary plea for the courage of suicide is certainly tension-provoking.

Or suppose we have a man whose family had sworn allegiance to one of the claimants to a European throne and had suffered grievously for it. Now suppose that allegiance is to be renounced. It can be a spine-tingling moment if it is done with high theatricality. In William Thackeray's 19th-century work, *Henry Esmond*, this is what takes place as Colonel Esmond revokes his allegiance to the Pretender:

"You will please, sir, to remember," he continued, "that my family hath ruined itself by fidelity to yours; that my grandfather spent his estate and gave his blood and his son to die in your service; that my dear lord's grandfather . . . died for the same cause; that my poor kinswoman, my father's second wife, after giving away her honor to your wicked perjured race, sent all her wealth to the King; and got in return that precious title that lies in ashes, and this inestimable yard of blue ribbon. I lay this at your feet and stamp upon it: I draw this sword and break it and deny you; and had you completed the wrong you designed us, by Heaven, I would have driven it through your heart. . . "

This is threat and anger, unmodified by other dialogue, yet establishing the scene and motivation. There is no need for another character to speak, there is no need to break up the speech for any other purpose. Esmond tells us why he feels the way he does, he tells us what he intends to do about it, he tells who he believes wronged him. The disagreement is there, of course, in the nature of Esmond's words, yet it's all done by monologue.

Is there any doubt we have tension? The anger's there, the disagreement is plain, and we certainly want to know what will happen next.

And it's obvious, to echo Trollope's words, that this dialogue contributes to the telling of the story. The storyline is certainly moved forward.

Sometimes, the most effective tension-building comes not so much from what the characters say to one another as from what they *don't* say. What they hold back, what they hide, brings the reader directly into the scene, assuming the reader knows what is being held back. The reader becomes a partner with the author, watching and judging reactions. Suppose, for example, one brother suspects another brother of a crime, but he knows he'll be lied to if he asks. He has to know, yet he can't come right out and ask:

"You got home late last night."

"Lousy driving, fog, the roads were slick."

"See the paper this morning?"

"Something I should know?"

"You ought to get home earlier. You look shot."

He laughs. "Ease up on the booze, you mean."

"I guess."

"Hey." He taps him on the shoulder. "Who's got the old man's booze talent in this family?"

"Look..."

"Gotta go," he says, rummaging in the closet for his coat. "What about the paper, anyway?"...

This is tension of the unsaid thought, which can be a powerful story-mover. Note how nothing was said about the crime or about the suspicion. Yet we feel the uncertainty.

Raymond Carver does this beautifully. In his short story, *What Is It?*, he has Leo on the phone with his wife whom he sent downtown to sell their convertible for cash. Leo needs the money desperately because he is bankrupt, and his wife calls him from a downtown restaurant. She is having dinner with a sales manager from a used car lot to whom she has sold the car, and the sales manager will drive her home. Leo is jealous and upset, but he doesn't want to show it:

"Honey?" he says. He holds the receiver against his ear and rocks back and forth, eyes closed.

"Honey?"

"I have to go," she says. "I wanted to call. Anyway, guess how much?"

"Honey?" he says.

"Six and a quarter," she says. "I have it in my purse. He said there's no market for convertibles. I guess we're born lucky," she says and laughs. "I told him everything I think I had to."

"Honey?" he says.

"What?" she says.

"Please honey," Leo says.

"He said he sympathized," she says. "But he would have said anything." She laughs again. "He said personally he'd rather be classified a robber or a rapist than a bankrupt. He's nice enough, though," she says.

"Come home," he says. "Take a cab and come home."

Does Leo shout or cry or scream? Does he warn his wife that the sales manager may be a threat to her or to both of them? Does Carver show Leo tight lipped with anger?

He has him plead, he has him suppress his feelings into one plaintive word—*honey*—and we know what he must be feeling. We squirm with his discomfort, yet how different it would be if Leo had shouted out his anger.

Which of the two methods produces the greater tension? In Carver's story Leo's struggle is really a double battle—he battles his wife, who seems not to be responding to his urgings, *and* he battles himself as he tries to suppress his true feelings. If he had shouted out his anger, then the battle would be limited to his wife, and a layer of tension would be wiped off.

But note the artistry—one word, *honey*, can accomplish so much.

The underplayed scene is a useful device for provoking tension because there is that double battle, and often the bigger struggle is the one of restraint. But underplaying a scene can be just as effective when nothing is held back. The tension of underplaying comes in the calmness of players against the exploding intensity of the atmosphere. The dangers lurk, but the characters don't back away from them. It is the tension of two conflicting circumstances.

Take Elmore Leonard, for example. His dialogue is well recognized for its brutal realism, its absorbing style. In *City Primeval*, he has his detective, Raymond, standing across a table from Clement, a vicious criminal who has challenged Raymond to an old-time shooting match—basically a quick draw. They are in a high-rise apartment, and they each have pistols, though Raymond has taken Clement's away from him and has it resting in the middle of the table. Notice the seeming rationality with which Raymond discusses the issue with Clement; notice, too, that Clement is not so calm:

"...This is fair, isn't it? You said, why don't we have a shooting match. Okay we're doing it."

"Just grab for the guns, huh?"

"Wait a minute," Raymond said. "No. I think the way we ought to do it—pick up the gun and hold it at your side. Go ahead. I think that'll be better." Raymond brought the Colt toward him and held it pointing down, the barrel extending below the edge of the desk. "Yeah, that's better. See, then when you bring it up, you have to clear the desk and there's less chance of getting shot in the balls."

"Come on," Clement said, "cut the shit."

"All right, then you reach for yours and I raise mine," Raymond said, "it's up to you." He waited...

It's a murderous scene, and at the least there should be sweat, heavy breathing, and the beginnings of terror. Someone is going to die.

But Raymond talks as if he's directing a bake sale. The calmness in the midst of excruciating uncertainty. The tension of opposite circumstances.

Try these examples:

- anger in the midst of peaceful tolerance;
- giddiness in the midst of unsmiling gravity;
- unscrupulousness in the midst of trusting acceptance.

We could develop dialogue for each of these situations, and we'd have a mirror image of what Elmore Leonard does. At least one of the characters reflects a point of view or a posture directly opposite to the general atmosphere. The tension of opposite circumstances.

The reader remains a key player in dialogue tension, and as with the Raymond Carver story, if the reader knows something one of the characters doesn't know, there's an element of suspense. This is especially true when what is unsaid becomes a reason for something happening. It becomes motivation, but only one of the characters knows it. The dialogue becomes an exchange between people on different levels, basically unresponsive.

Deborah Singmaster shows this well in her story, *The Burial*, set in Ireland. Pat and Maureen have been engaged to be married for four years. Pat meets an exciting young woman on the beach and follows her into the dunes where they make love. Father Sullivan, newly arrived in the parish, comes upon them, but says nothing. Two weeks later Pat and Maureen are married, and then, years later, Father Sullivan dies and Pat drives the hearse containing the body. Somehow the hearse goes off the road and the coffin plunges into the sea with all the mourners watching. It is a few moments later. . .

> Maureen looked at him, trying to catch his eye. Pat avoided her gaze, he was staring down at the mud one moment and up at the sky the next, blinking as if there were sunlight pouring down on him.
>
> "Look at me," she said, keeping her voice low. Pat looked at her. He was grinning. Behind him the men were heaving the hearse back on the track. Maureen said, "That was no accident, was it? You did it on purpose, didn't you?"
>
> "And why would I do a thing like that?"
>
> "God alone knows, for what harm did he ever do you, Pat Riordan?"
>
> "What indeed."
>
> Maureen turned her back on her husband and walked up the hill to join the other mourners. . .

The only thing Maureen really knows is that things aren't quite right. She doesn't know why, and she doesn't know how. Just that her husband allowed the priest's body to find a watery grave, clearly a violation of ordered civility.

But Pat knows. And the reader knows. The why of it is simple retribution. Would he have married Maureen if the priest hadn't spotted him in the dunes? Was his short leap for freedom aborted? Has he blamed the priest for his dull, conventional life with Maureen?

Especially when he had tasted what life *could* be like, however briefly?

Singmaster doesn't spell it out for us. But the inferences are clear. And so is the motivation. Singmaster has Pat playing dumb to his wife's inquisition, but we, the readers, know that he has collected a debt.

Unsaid, unmentioned.

The essence of dialogue tension, of course, is in the words we use. Certain words or phrases create tension, such as he *barked*, she *screamed*, he *shouted*, she *slapped*...verbs, in other words, that signify action or anger or some aspect of conflict. There are nouns, too, that get the job done. When we talk about *hate, fear, death, bully, winner* and *loser, criminal*, we are setting a certain mark on the page that must be countered. For example, if someone is a bully, there must be someone else to push around, and the very nature of the relationship leads to tension and conflict. Or if we call someone a criminal, then something unlawful—perhaps even terrible—must have happened. An automatic two-sides question, the good guys and the bad guys. The word "criminal" implies this from its very appearance on the page.

The importance of careful selection of words and phrases that promote tension and conflict must be emphasized. The words, themselves, set up the scene and carry it forward. The words are the foundation blocks. If we have one character call another "pleasant, delightful, enjoyable" we have no tension; if we have the same character growl that the other is a "yellow-spined coward, mean spirited and a thief," we have tension, for sure.

Take John Updike. Many of his scenes are set in mannered circumstances. There is general politeness, and usually an air of civility. How does he create tension without at the same time dissolving the entire scene into chaos? He uses tension-producing words, and he lays emphasis in certain places. Words and emphasis, a good combination.

In his story, *Marry Me*, he has two couples in a showdown over the affair between Jerry (married to Ruth) and Sally (married to Richard). Sally and Ruth are having it out with husbands looking on. Sally is speaking...

"...I've cried plenty on your account. I feel sorry for anybody who's so selfish, who's so weak she won't let a man go when he wants to go."

"I tried to hold my children's father with them. Was that so contemptible?"

"Yes!"

"You can say that because you treat your own children like, like baggage, like little trinkets to set you off when it suits you."

"I love my children, but I have respect for my husband, too, enough respect that if he made up his mind I'd let him do what he decided."

"Jerry never decided anything."

"He's too *kind*. You abused that kindness. You used it. You can't give him what I can give him, you don't love him."...

"Girls, girls," Richard said...

Sally cries...feels sorry...she accuses Ruth of selfishness, weakness, of abusing kindness, of using it...she can give Jerry more...

Ruth accuses Sally of treating her children like baggage...like trinkets...she puts Jerry down because he never decided anything...

Simple words and phrases, but they carry the seeds of conflict. Updike pits the women against each other, not in any violent manner but with sharp, civilized thrusts. Note that he emphasizes the word "affair," giving it a greater significance thereby. The fact of it might have been missed, if he hadn't emphasized it. So he uses it as an additional epithet, as a highly charged tension-producer. "Affair" is not only a description here, it is also a characterization. That "affair" means an immoral event only an especially immoral person would undertake. It's the same as criticizing someone who treats children like baggage.

Words and emphasis, they can accomplish the same thing.

And dialogue tension can be substantially enhanced along the way.

2

Would He/She Say That?

"Her voice is full of money," Jay Gatsby says, describing Daisy Buchanan in F. Scott Fitzgerald's *The Great Gatsby*. Does that build an image for us, can we picture what Fitzgerald means? *Her voice is full of money!* When Daisy speaks, it tells us things about her, she becomes more than a walk-on character, she has a distinction we remember.

It tells us she is rich, it tells us she doesn't hide the fact she is rich.

And if she's rich, other characteristics flow: self-confidence, good taste, easy gratification.

Her voice is full of money!

Dialogue is an essential ingredient for the portrayal and development of character. Narrative describes a character but dialogue humanizes and personifies the character. It gives dimension and substance and individuality. "We all sound different, use different words, expressions, euphemisms, dialects, speech styles and varied inflections," wrote Robyn Carr some years ago. "*What* we say, *how* we say it, *when* we choose to speak reflects who we really are."

Dialogue, then, must be fashioned in the manner of a sculptor molding a piece of clay. It must individualize the speaker, and it must be something that speaker would say. For example, we wouldn't have a character with a limited education hold forth on highly technical matters, nor would we have an elderly person speak in the jargon of a teenager. These, of course, are extreme examples, and the real dilemma a writer faces is to draw more subtle distinctions such as:

- the reaction of a single mother to criticism of her child by her new lover; would it be anger, excuse-making, guilt?
- the reaction of a quiet, studious young man to unexpected honors; would it be boastfulness, modesty, withdrawal?

Would she/he say that? An important thing to remember. In the case of the single mother, her first reaction might be to defend her child, without thinking of the divisive effect it could have on the relationship with her lover. "He didn't mean it like that!" is one thing she could say. "He's tried to do things the way you want!" is another way. Make her defensive, make her uneasy with her lover's criticism, especially directed at her child. The mother stays in character, and the story moves.

As for the young man, his reaction would seem to be more consistent with modesty or withdrawal. "Why couldn't they mail the plaque and check? I hate speeches," is one reaction he could have. His withdrawal might be silence or unavailability or tearful avoidance. He could say or do these things and still remain in character.

Would she/he say that?

One of the more useful techniques for dialogue is to have one character talk about another, give us clues to that other's personality. Remember Jay Gatsby's description of Daisy Buchanan? *Her voice is full of money* . . . when Daisy speaks we remember what Gatsby says.

David Kranes does the same thing in his story, *Dealer*, about a man, Hatch, an expert dealer of cards at a Nevada gaming club. Hatch rarely loses, and like the gunfighter of the Old West, he has a reputation that attracts people who try to beat him. One night a woman comes to his table to play, and later Hatch runs into her at the bar:

"You're very good," she said.

Hatch nodded.

"Buy me a drink?"

Hatch held his hand up. The bartender came. Hatch pointed at the bartender for the girl.

"I'll have a whiskey sour, please," she said.

The bartender moved off.

"I'll bet you're a very cruel man," she said, her voice uneven. "The way you deal. There's something very . . .

"I just deal," Hatch told her.

"No you don't." Something approached a smile on her lips. "No you don't. No."

Three things happen here, each brought out in the woman's words. *You're very good*, she says, and this reaffirms the fact that he *is* good. Hatch is a very good dealer, and the woman says so. Then she says, *I'll bet you're a very cruel man*. This is a new thought, barely hinted at up to now. Would a hot dealer be a cruel man? We could make a case for it . . . unemotional, opportunistic, unkind, strongly competitive. It takes all of these things—and more—to make a successful card dealer. One ounce of compassion and the dealer loses the edge.

So when the woman calls him cruel, we can be pretty sure she's got him pegged.

The third thing the woman does is to disagree with his "aw-shucks" self-description. *No you don't*, she says, *No you don't. No.*

This reinforces her description of him as cruel. In repeating her statement, she is adding something else: when he said *I just deal*, and she disagrees, the sense of it is much more significant. The woman is tipping us off, even though she doesn't offer anything more, and it encourages us to read on and find out.

One short passage is all it takes. One character describing another, and a solid mental image emerges.

Hatch is a very good dealer; he's cruel, and he's more, much more, than his self-effacing self-description tells us.

Sometimes, the character being described does not even have to be present. "Let me tell you what I found out about Henry..." a conversation can go. "He's the man with the puffy red cheeks and the lopsided grin. You can't miss him..."

Men get together and talk about women, women talk about men, even though the opposite sexes are not present. We can call it gossip or a bull session, but it does develop character, it can describe and illuminate. And once in a while we meet a descriptive passage of dialogue that lifts us beyond the usual. It is uncommon enough to set an example.

Such is *Mrs. Bathurst*, a story by Rudyard Kipling set at the turn of the century. British army enlisted personnel are talking about their favorite subject—women—and as they talk, the name of Mrs. Bathurst comes up. Note how her character is portrayed, especially in contrast to the men's attitude toward other women:

> Said Pyecroft suddenly: "How many women have you been intimate with all over the world, Pritch?"
>
> Pritchard blushed plum color to the short hairs of his seventeen-inch neck.
>
> "'Undreds," said Pyecroft. "So've I. How many of 'em can you remember in your own mind, settin' aside the first—and' perhaps the last—*and one more?*"
>
> "Few, wonderful few, now I tax myself," said Sergeant Pritchard, relieved.
>
> "An' how many times might you've been at Auckland?"
>
> "One-two," he began. "Why, I can't make it more than three times in ten years. But I can remember every time I saw Mrs. B."

"So can I—and' I've only been in Auckland twice—how she stood an' what she was sayin', an' what she looked like. That's the secret. 'Tisn't beauty, so to speak, nor good talk necessarily. It's just It. Some women'll stay in a man's memory if they once walked down the street..."

The curious thing about this story is that Mrs. Bathurst never appears. She remains a vivid memory to all, nothing more. She has "It," and Kipling is smart enough not to get more specific. "It" can mean what each of us wants it to mean, something important, something sexy, something desirable. "It" is personal and individual, though no less effective. "It" is significant and Mrs. Bathurst materializes in our minds, doesn't she?

And when she is contrasted with the other women—who clearly don't have "It"—she becomes even more significant.

Mrs. Bathurst isn't the only one being developed here; the soldiers, themselves, are portrayed. By learning what they feel is important in a woman, we learn what they might be like. What they find attractive, in other words, is what gives us clues to their characters.

Suppose, though, we turn it around and look at attraction from the woman's perspective. What is it that a woman finds attractive in a man, and how does the woman say it? If the soldiers in Kipling's story look for "It," what might a woman look for?

In *The Moon and Sixpence*, W. Somerset Maugham's lengthy saga of the trials of club-footed Philip Carey and his barely requited love for the elusive Mildred, we see a portrayal of a different kind. Mildred is talking with Philip about herself and she lets us glimpse her in provocative fashion. We learn a bit of her background and her standards for judging men:

"I was not fifteen when my father found that I had a lover," she said. "He was third mate on the *Tropic Bird*. A good-looking boy."

She sighed a little. They say a woman always remembers her first lover with affection; but perhaps she does not always remember him.

"My father was a sensible man."

"What did he do?" I asked.

"He thrashed me within an inch of my life, and then he made me marry Captain Johnson. I did not mind. He was older, of course, but he was good-looking, too."

For Mildred "good-looking" is the operative phrase. It became sufficient motivation for her to enter a teenaged marriage without resentment. What can this tell us about her?

Three things at least:

- she was a sexually precocious fifteen-year-old;
- superficial good looks were sufficient justification for almost anything;
- she held no anger towards her father for forcing the marriage.

When we translate this into how the adult Mildred speaks and behaves, we see her as experienced, confident with men, and still highly charged with sexuality. When Maugham gives us a portrait of Mildred as a fifteen-year-old, he's providing reasons why, later in life, she might treat the bumbling, uncertain attentions of Philip with disdain. Mildred has been *around*, and her words and manner of speaking mirror this. What she says as an adult we expect, from the way she described herself as a teenager.

"A "good-looking" man turned her on when she was young. Would it be any different now that she is older?

An important consideration with most fiction is that the characters—or at least the main characters—grow or change as the story moves along. If characters remain static, they become dull, and page after page the reader can only look forward to more of the same. Character *rigor mortis* has set in.

Lively dialogue, however, can bring on character development and show changes happening right before the reader. Characters may grow kinder, wiser, angrier, meaner, healthier ...and they provide the evidence through their own words. We don't have to tell the reader these things happen, we can show them taking place:

"I don't think I want to sell my uncle's drawings."

"Two months ago you begged me to buy them."

"My mother died last week. I've no family now."

A character changing before our eyes, becoming something different, acquiring different values. The reader has to be interested because the story will change. The expected is now the unexpected, and the other characters will have to adjust.

A recent literary example of this is a conversation between father and son in Louis Auchincloss's novel, *Honorable Men*. Chip Benedict, the son, is about to enter law school and he has decided he wants more control over his financial affairs. He has directed the bank trust officer to send him whatever money is due from family trusts and not to pay it over to his father as has been done. His father invites him to the Yale Club to discuss it:

"...But are you sure, my boy, that you're acting in your own best interests? I thought you and I had agreed that I should handle any money settled on you for tax reasons while you were busy being educated."

"I've changed my mind. That is, if I ever really made it up. From now on, I'll be my own boss."

"You don't consider that you may hold money that your mother and I gave you in a kind of moral trust?"

"I don't see how a money trust can be moral. But of course I understand what you're driving at. You'd be entirely justified in disinheriting me. Go ahead..."

Chip Benedict is making a strike for independence, he is changing, he is no longer the dutiful son. He is challenging his father, offering to take the consquences if his father picks up the challenge. This is not the same young man who went about his days contentedly aware that Daddy would take care of things. Chip Benedict has become a different character, and the writer's task now becomes to portray him in this manner.

Two questions must be dealt with:

- how does he react with the other characters—what changes in their relationships take place?
- how will the story itself be changed—what will happen now?

One thing only can we be confident about: an independent Chip Benedict will have a pervasive influence in both areas.

All because a character changed. Doesn't it fit Trollope's words: *dialogue should contribute to the telling of the story*!

From rational, gentlemanly behavior, dialogue can certainly produce highly-charged circumstances. Neither Chip Benedict nor his father raises his voice. Their manners are most civilized, yet Chip offers a profound alternative—disinheritance. The passions are there—they are only subdued.

But the passion need not be hidden. Dialogue can show changes in character in the midst of electric emotion. Ernest Hemingway portrays this well in *The Sun Also Rises*, his story of American expatriates in Europe following World War I. Jake Barnes, the sexually impotent hero, is speaking with Brett Ashley about a young bullfighter both have come to know. Jake is clearly in love with Brett who is compulsive, neurotic, and obviously in an agitated frame of mind.

"Do you still love me, Jake?"

"Yes," I said.

"Because I'm a goner," Brett said.

"How?"

"I'm a goner. I'm mad about the Romero boy. I'm in love with him, I think."

"I wouldn't be if I were you."

"I can't help it. I'm a goner. It's tearing me all up inside."

"Don't do it."

"I can't help it. I've never been able to help anything."

"You ought to stop it."

"How can I stop it? I can't stop things. Feel that."

Her hand was trembling.

"I'm like that all through."

"You oughtn't to do it."

"I can't help it. I'm a goner anyway . . ."

Brett is changing here. Through her own words we see her admitting a weakness and an inability to cope. She is asking for help, yet saying at the same time that she is beyond help. Note her words: *I'm a goner*. . .she says it four times, and we see that now she is a different person than she was before she fell for the bullfighter.

The character's own words tell us the change is taking place.

The passion and the excrutiating discomfort of the event keep us interested.

Dialogue is the key. The characters come to life.

Keep these items in mind:

- *know the characters* (their habits, backgrounds, points of view);
- *understand the characters' motivations* (why they say what they say);
- *make the characters consistent* (don't have them saying uncharacteristic things).

Dialogue writing must illuminate character development, not suppress it. Consider the following:

"I would hardly expect you to understand my reasons," he said.

"I'm not going to listen," she said.

"Slut!" He backhanded her across the room.

Does the man stay in character? Is there motivation for his striking the woman? Do we know why he gets angry?

Doesn't his response really hide the fact that there might be cogent explanations for why he has no faith in her understanding? If the man were allowed to remain consistent, we might learn more about him and more about the story.

Wouldn't a better response from him be:

"Ever since we were ten years old, you've believed that crazy story Aunt Minerva spread. . ."

What crazy story, we ask? How does it bear on this incident, and what will happen next?

This is character development, not suppression, and the story moves along.

Suppose we have a scene with more than two characters, and each is different enough so that individual dialogue passages have to be distinctive. We have to write so that readers will be able to identify who is speaking, even if there are no modifiers or descriptive aids.

Ken Kesey performs this sort of thing with his story of life in a mental institution, *One Flew Over the Cuckoo's Nest*. Note in the following passage how he sticks to the rules about knowing his characters and their motivations. Note, too, that by their words we know who is speaking at any moment.

We have three characters: McMurphy, the irrepressible, con-man rebel; Harding the defeated intellectual; and Billy, the wishy-washy good boy. The issue is whether they will badger Nurse Ratched to turn on the World Series even though it will change the routine in the ward.

> "I tell ya, I can't figure it out. Harding, what's wrong with *you* for crying out loud? You afraid if you raise your hand that old buzzard'll cut it off?"
>
> Harding lifts one thin eyebrow. "Perhaps I am perhaps I *am* afraid she'll cut it off if I raise it."
>
> "What about you, Billy? Is that what you're scared of?"
>
> "No, I don't think she'd d-d-*do* anything, but"—he shrugs and sighs and climbs up on the big panel that controls the nozzles on the shower. Perches up there like a monkey—"but I just don't think a vote wu-wu-would do any good. Not in the l-long run. It's just no use, M-mack."
>
> "Do any *good*? Hooee! It'd do you birds some good just to get the exercise lifting that arm."
>
> "It's still a risk, my friend. She always has the capacity to make things worse for us. A baseball game isn't worth the risk," Harding says.
>
> "Who the hell says so? Jesus, I haven't missed a World Series in years . . ."

Even if Kesey had left off the descriptive modifier in each passage, we would know who was speaking. McMurphy is clearly defined, as are Harding and Billy. Each one shows us a side of himself consistent with the general portrait already put together. We see McMurphy trying to rally the inmates, and his rebellious con-man instincts shine through; we see Harding, admitting fear of Nurse Ratched, showing defeat even before the battle is started; we see Billy, unable to muster any strong enthusiasm even though he might give the project some personal support. His stutter adds to his uncertainty.

It comes back, then, to one simple phrase. *Would she/he say that?*

If the answer is yes, character development flows.

If the answer is no, the dialogue lessons haven't been well learned.

3

Where Am I?

A writer friend once remarked, "Whenever I'm stuck how to begin a piece, I fall back on the weather." *It was a sparkling fall day, and the breeze had a touch of chill* . . .

His technique. Overworked, perhaps, but it does get him going. By the time he finishes, the story may be much different, and the opening may have been discarded. Yet there is something special in what he does.

It's a simple principle: *technique opens the writing door*!

Technique. Method. The way we do something. For my writer friend, a descriptive passage about the weather will start the creative juices flowing. For each of us it might be something different. But techniques—which we can learn—not only speed up the writing process, they can precipitate it as well.

The way we set a story or set a scene is especially determined by technique. There are methods for setting a story, and they aid in creating mood or atmosphere. We must answer the simple question, *where am I*? We look at it geographically, temporally (is the story contemporaneous, in the past or in the future?), culturally, socially. Are we in London? If so, we must set the story to reflect that. No strange events or people or physical presence that might be found only in New York. Are we with a poor white immigrant family? We wouldn't have them talking with college-educated voices, nor would we have them speculating on happenings beyond their sphere of interest. Are we developing atmosphere heavy with politics? We'd encourage pragmatism, partisanship, loud speaking, heavy body odors...

Where Am I? We answer by setting the scene.

Remember my writer friend. His technique called for a narrative approach. It needn't be this way, however. Dialogue is just as valuable a tool for scene-setting, and in some ways it is more useful than narrative because it won't bog the reader down in long paragraphs. People talk about where they are and what they are doing just as easily as we can describe what is going on.

See the difference:

This is narrative:

> The city had a cold feel, even though it was midsummer and the sun hung like a searing eye...

This is dialogue:

> "I've got to make a train in ten minutes."
>
> "I'm off duty," the cabby said.
>
> "But your light's on. I need help..."
>
> "Yeah?" the cabbie reached under his dash and flipped off the light. He resumed reading his paper...

Both approaches set the scene, but the one with dialogue adds dimension—there's conflict and emotion. The narrative tells us what the dialogue shows us. *Where Am I?* becomes a vivid portrayal.

The techniques through dialogue for setting the scene are numerous, and in one of the most frequently used, the characters comment upon and judge their surroundings. They talk about what they see, and the reader sees it through their eyes. Here's William Faulkner, in *Light In August*, writing about two white farmers watching a poor white girl, Lena, trudging up the dusty road past them.

> While Armstid and Winterbottom were squatting

against the shady wall of Winterbottom's stable, they saw her pass in the road. They saw at once that she was young, pregnant and a stranger. "I wonder where she got that belly," Winterbottom said.

"I wonder how far she has brought it afoot," Armstid said.

"Visiting somebody back down the road, I reckon," Winterbottom said.

"I reckon not. Or I would have heard. And it ain't nobody up my way neither. I would have heard that, too."

"I reckon she knows where she's going," Winterbottom said. "She walks like it."

"She'll have company, before she goes much further..."

As they speculate about where Lena is going and where she came from, both farmers show us the face of the rural south—sparsely settled (they claim to know who is visiting whom at any time), suspicious of strangers (what's a pregnant girl doing on this road, on foot?), with horse-sense judgment (she knows where she's going, she walks like it).

The general atmosphere is one of curiosity and suspicion, but we sense other things—a dusty road, hot sun, grizzled farmers' faces, a whiff of sexuality. This is all part of setting the scene, even though in the passage above not one word of narrative is used to describe the landscape or the appearance of the characters or even the weather! Not one word.

Yet as Armstid and Winterbottom discuss and judge Lena, we have a feel for how it looks and how it seems.

Conflict, as we saw earlier, can always set a mood, but we have to be careful about what type of conflict—what type of mood—we want to create. It wouldn't do, for example, to set a conflict when the mood we are trying to convey is one of harmony and peace. On the other hand, conflict can be useful to show the bittersweet aspects of an unfamiliar way of life. It is another technique for setting a scene or story, and as we develop the conflict, the setting itself emerges in multi-dimension.

Consider, for example, an exotic wedding service on an island in the South Pacific. If the mood is to be peaceful, we certainly wouldn't have conflict, and we'd probably describe the wedding using narration in order to set the scene. We'd get a feeling for the way people live.

But if peace and harmony are not key, then conflict could erupt during the ceremony, and by means of dialogue we could get just as good an idea of how the people lived and the way they thought.

Where am I? could be answered with either approach. But think how much more dramatic conflict and dialogue could be; again, it's a case of showing rather than telling.

Have a good look at Alice Walker's novel, *Meridian*, the story of a young black girl in the south, trying to cope with her own feelings about civil rights (she has joined the "Movement") and the promise of a better life even while she has become a teenaged mother. She gets a chance to attend college through the generosity of a wealthy white family, and she must give up her young son, Eddie, Jr., to do so. She goes to tell her mother, accompanied by Delores, a friend in the Movement.

"You should *want* Eddie, Jr.," said Mrs. Hill. "Unless you're some kind of monster. And no daughter of mine is a monster, surely."

Meridian closed her eyes as tight as she could.

Delores cleared her throat. "The only way Meridian can take care of Eddie Jr. is if she moves in here with you and gets a job in somebody's kitchen while you take care of the kid."

"Of course I'll help out," said Mrs. Hill. "I wouldn't let either of 'em starve, but—" she continued speaking to Delores as if Meridian were not present,—"This is a clean, upright *Christian* home. We believe in God in this house."

"What's that got to do with anything?" asked Delores, whose face expressed belligerence and confusion. "The last time God had a baby he skipped, too."

This is generational conflict, as well as a philosophical one.

The new, young, upwardly mobile black woman against the status-quo conscious, strict moral-fibered older black woman. But don't we also get a glimmer of the way these people live? Alice Walker sets the scene by portraying a disagreement over whether to give the baby away, and this, in itself, shows us motivation. Meridian will give her baby away so she can attend college. Is college that important? Should it be that important? Mrs. Hill obviously doesn't think so, but then she's from the old school. Meridian and Delores think it's appropriate, and in this we see the blossoming of a black urge for upward mobility. But what a price to pay!

Doesn't this tell us a lot about these characters, the way they live and what they consider to be important? Isn't the conflict really about values and how the people cope? If we understand the motivations of these characters, can't we visualize the pain and the anger and the impatience and the insults?

Do we need a narrative to describe the physical setting, to emphasize the feelings on each face? I don't think so. The dialogue itself should be sufficient.

Conflict, then, is a technique for establishing setting. Almost as a corollary to conflict is another technique which follows a similar pattern. Call it contrast, and the more vivid the better. Contrast, not conflict.

Contrast is evident when at least one person in the scene doesn't seem in harmony with the background of the scene. When, for example, an exotic-looking woman steps from a lifeboat filled with shipwreck survivors or a well-known baseball player wears earrings or, as in Richard Condon's *Prizzi's Honor*, a hired killer is a lovely female. Contrast is evident when we have that out-of-place character speaking and acting in such a way as to inject more adrenalin into the scene's portrayal. The baseball player wearing earrings, for example, can still talk baseball, but even as he discourses, we visualize his earrings and the bizarre effect they have on the other characters:

> "Jesus, these new earrings pinch." He massaged his ear lobe.

"Your arm strong enough to go seven today?" the skipper asked.

"Howie says I'll blow 'em away."

Sunlight glinted from the dangling gold designs. The skipper faced the outfield. "No self respectin'. . . ."

Contrast and conflict are similar as tools for setting a scene. Both rely on the attraction of opposites, but there are differences. With conflict there is contention and antagonism. People are at odds. This doesn't have to be the case with contrast. There *may* be conflict, but there doesn't have to be. Contrast may be merely different shadings or varied approaches. People don't have to be in contention for there to be contrast.

Consider the following. It's Philip Caputo's *Del Corso's Gallery*, the story of war photo-journalists working first in Viet Nam and then in Beirut. Bolton, one of the characters, is in Beirut near the Green Line separating Christian and Moslem militias. He wants to make a call back to his editors, and he is taken to an upper floor of a building where a telephone is available. He enters the room only to see a dark-eyed, beautiful woman at the window holding a rifle and leaning against sandbags. She looks at him:

"So. You are a journalist."

"Yeah."

"American?"

"Right."

"I thought so."

"What do you mean, you thought so?"

"I guessed you were an American."

"I don't get it."

"You live on the eighth floor of the Mazzan Building."

A faint, uncomfortable buzz traveled up and down Bolton's spine.

"This," she said, pointing with a lacquered fingernail at the scope of her Winchester. "There are all Moslems in your building. The first time I saw you, through the jalousies, I was that close"—the finger with which she'd pointed closed to within a hair's breadth of her thumb—"but then I saw your light hair and how tall you are and I knew you could not be an Arab..."

Do we smell the atmosphere, do we get a sense of the scene? Would it have been as effective if the person holding the rifle had been a dusty, grubby militiaman? Doesn't the horror of the scene become vivid because a beautiful woman with lacquered fingernails holds a rifle and casually admits she almost killed Bolton because he happened to come into her sights?

The point to understand is the contrast here. War and destruction are not so unique that a writer can paint them with complete singularity. But if one of the participants—in this case a beautiful woman—is active and deadly, then the war setting becomes a little different, and memorable.

Suppose we want to create a sinister mood, one that crackles with suspense yet is carried out with the characters acting in normal fashion. Suppose, further, that our mood is not dependent on how people speak but on what they say... against a backdrop of eerie goings-on.

The people don't speak strangely, the people don't act strangely. But *something* is happening...

See Stephen King. See especially his work, *Pet Sematary*. Stephen King, the master of horror and weird occurrences, devises a story that takes place in a small Maine town. Louis Creed, his wife, and their children have moved from Chicago. Louis is a doctor and his nearest neighbor is 83-year-old Jud Crandall. One day, shortly after they move in, Jud tells them there is a pet cemetery in the woods behind their house. Local people have been burying their pets there for years. Jud takes Louis and his family to see it.

The mood is somber, as Louis stares at the cemetery.

"How far do these go back?"

"Gorry, I don't know," Jud said, putting his hands deep in his pockets. "Place was here when Spot died, of course. I had a whole gang of friends in those days. They helped me dig the hole for Spot. Digging here ain't that easy, either—ground's awful stoney, you know, hard to turn. And I helped them sometimes.'' He pointed here and there with a horney finger. ''That there was Pete LaVasseur's dog, if I remember right, and there's three of Albion Groatley's barncats buried right in a row there.

''Old man Fritchie kept racing pigeons. Me and Al Groatley and Carl Hannah buried one of them that a dog got. He's right there.'' He paused thoughtfully. ''I'm the last of that bunch left, you know. All dead now, my gang. All gone.''

Louis said nothing, only stood looking at the pet graves with his hands in his pockets.

''Ground's stoney,'' Jud repeated. ''Couldn't plant nothing here but corpses, anyway. . .''

The setting and mood are clearly sinister. It's Stephen King at his best. But note how he uses dialogue to develop the setting. He uses eerie words and phrases. . .*died. . .dig the hole. . .horney finger. . .buried. . .all dead. . .all gone. . . graves. . .corpses*. . .and everything is in relation to the pet cemetery they are standing around. The dialogue and the place interact to form the mood, and we know that something weird will happen.

It's technique, of course. If we want a sinister mood, we put sinister words in the mouths of our characters, and we place them in a sinister location.

It can work with other categories of fiction, as well. Suppose we want a mood and setting for romance? We wouldn't use words like *corpse* or *buried*, we'd speak of beauty and love and excitement and even joy. The people wouldn't be standing around a pet cemetery, they'd be lunching at Salmagundi's in San Francisco or cruising the canals of Venice in the starry moonlight. They'd speak of the joy of tender touching, the thrill of sparkling eyes.

In short, the words we use and the location where we speak

them should go hand-in-hand. They form a team, especially when we wish to develop a mood and enhance our setting.

Ernest Hebert does this well in a scene from his book, *The Dogs of March*. The story is set in New Hampshire, and it deals with poorly educated Howard Elman's daily battle to survive in a hostile world. What Hebert has done is to develop Stephen King's use of individual words a bit further. Not only can words create a mood but Hebert uses sounds to do the same thing. The sounds lend substance to the setting and characterize it.

Elman and his family are at Thanksgiving dinner with friends, Parker and Charlene Harris. Elman's son, Freddie, is there, wearing a beard which Elman doesn't approve of. In this scene, note how the sounds develop disorder, commotion, and general chaos.

"Houp, houp, houp, houp," Presently, Parker laughed at Freddie's beard.

Freddie suffered the laugh in silent anger, but his father tried half-heartedly to come to his defense.

"Parker will you pipe down so the rest of us can eat," he shouted.

Charlene gave Howard a vicious look.

"Charlene!" bellowed Howard.

"It's his house. He can say what he pleases," said Charlene.

"He don't say nothing. He just goes haw-haw," said Howard in a poor imitation of Parker's whooping cough laugh.

"Don't pick on him," said Charlene.

"You both pick," said Elenore, almost as an aside.

"Houp, houp, houp, houp." The tears came, and Parker almost fell off his chair, and he laughed all the more at himself. . .

Do we know where we are in this scene? Isn't it a usual holiday meal turned topsy-turvy by bickering and insensitivity and impatience? Where's the holiday spirit? Where could it be in the face of a whooping laugh that drowns out conversation and seems pointed at another's appearance?

Sounds. That's Ernest Hebert's technique, and it portrays a mood well, precipitating disorder which then characterizes the less-than-satisfying nature of the holiday meal.

Sounds. Anyone can create them.

Suppose we want to illuminate a broad principle, something beyond a simple character trait or physical setting. We want to highlight something that has become the general theme for what we are writing. The techniques we've already discussed could be appropriate, but perhaps we want something even simpler.

What about. . .questions and answers! One character questions, another answers and explains. It is dialogue directed to a specific end, that of presenting a general theme or overall point of view. The book, rather than the scene, is set in this way, and we learn where the author is coming from.

Consider this patch of dialogue from Ernest Hemingway's World War I novel, *A Farewell to Arms*. Lieutenant Henry has deserted his ambulance unit on the Italian front and fled with Catherine Barkley, a British nurse with whom he has fallen in love. They are trying to make the Swiss border, and they have come to a hotel in Northern Italy where they stop briefly. Henry relaxes by playing billiards with Count Greffi, an aged Italian. They are alone.

> "What do you think of war, really?" I asked.
> "I think it is stupid."
> "Who will win it?"
> "Italy."
> "Why?"
> "They are a younger nation."
> "Do younger nations always win wars?"
> "They are apt to for a time."
> "Then what happens?"
> "They become older nations."

"You said you were not wise."

"Dear boy, that is not wisdom, that is cynicism."

"It sounds very wise to me."

"It's not particularly. I could quote you the examples on the other side. But it is not bad . . .

An anti-war theme sharply articulated and driven home by the sparse dialogue. In the book, of course, Hemingway delves into the anti-war aspects a number of times, but the passage above is a particularly acute example. Note the question-and-answer technique. There is no attempt to characterize the speakers or to provide them with special motives. The characters, really, are just vehicles for an anti-war presentation, and the important thing to keep in mind is how this contributes to the general theme of the book.

Suppose we ask the basic question. . .*where am I*? In Hemingway's scene, the physical location is not important; but we know we're contending with anti-war sentiment. That is the general setting for the book.

Anti-war is the book's theme.

It's also the garden from which the story grows.

Where am I? Weighing the value of anti-war views.

Learning through questions and answers.

The simplest technique, really.

4

What's Happening?

The plot. It's the essence of any story. Without it there *is* no story.

Suppose we recast *Alice in Wonderland*:

"What's the plot supposed to do?" asked Alice.

"No, no, you have it wrong," said the King of Hearts.

"Wrong?"

"The plot, you see, doesn't do anything. Other things do to it. Of course you see that!"

"The plot *is* the story," said Alice, not so sure.

"No, no, the story is the plot."

"Why, that's the same thing."

"Oh, no," grinned the King, "move the plot, push it, shove it, twist it. Only then is the story tellable."

"Poor plot, it must hurt to be pushed around."

"Plots are used to it..."

We think of the plot of a story as a blueprint for the action, and in a simplified way that's probably so. The plot does indeed carry the main theme of the story, and other elements in the tale must reflect from it. The plot tells us what happens, when and where it happens and how it happens. The characters usually tell us why it happens.

The plot, however, is never static. It is constantly in motion, bringing the story to its resolution. The steps through which the plot moves are the result of a character or group of characters doing or saying things that cause other things to happen.

That is why the King can tell Alice that other things can *do* to the plot and not the other way around.

Anger moves the plot, for instance, as do greed and jealousy. Search and ambition move the plot; fear and horror do, too. The writer can narrate page after page of circumstances that carry the story forward. His effort can be replete with description and action and line after line of story involvement.

Or he can accomplish the same thing with dialogue.

Poor plot, it must hurt to be pushed around...

Dialogue can push the plot around. It can move the story. Consider this passage from Loren D. Estleman's western novel, *Murdock's Law*:

"What's your business?"

"Page Murdock. I wired you last week from Helena looking for a Deane-Adams. You said you had one."

"Hell of a long ride just for a gun."

"I was coming anyway."

His eyes narrowed. "You some kind of law?"

"Does it show?"

"You could be on one side or the other, from the look of you. In this business I see my share of both."

"Maybe you've seen Chris Shedwell lately," I said. "My boss got a report he's on his way here. He's wanted for a mail train robbery near Wichita ten years ago..."

Note that almost every line of dialogue pushes the story along. Nothing is wasted or non-informational. Murdock has only four individual speeches and look what he tells us:

- he already had plans to come to town;
- he admits he's a lawman;
- he's looking for Chris Shedwell, a train robber who is on his way to town;
- he wired ahead looking for a special gun.

Each of these speeches nudges the plot. They tell us things we didn't know, and they add substance to the story. After reading the short passage, we know more about what's happening than we did before.

Another example is from Bobbi Ann Mason's recent work, *Incountry*, the story of Kentucky hill people coming to grips with the final memories of Viet Nam. For Sam, a teenaged girl, the memories are blank because her father went overseas before she was born and never returned. She wants to know about him and approaches her grandmother, Mamaw:

"Did any stuff come with the body?" Sam asked. "I mean like his personal stuff. His clothes and things?"

Mamaw nodded. "There wasn't much. I gave away the clothes, and I made Irene take the flag, but she wouldn't take anything else. I didn't understand that."

"Mom said there might be a notebook."

"There was a little diary. It's around here somewhere."

"Do you care if I have it?"

"I can't imagine what you want with it. There's not much in it. He told more in his letters. He wrote the lovingest letters. I wouldn't take anything for them. But I'll look for that notebook..."

Here again, we're finding out things we didn't know before. Most of the information comes from Mamaw in response to Sam's questions (and of course, the question-and-answer technique is useful for prodding the plot). Mamaw tells us:

- how she disposed of her son's effects;
- that there's a diary;
- that her son's letters were more impressive;
- that Sam can have the diary if she wants it.

Note that here, as with Loren Estleman's work, almost every line of dialogue moves the story along. From Sam's initial question about the existence of the diary to Mamaw's agreeing to look for it, we have substance being added to the plot and the story itself moving forward.

What's happening? Sam wants to find the diary. Mamaw says she has it, Mamaw says she'll give it to Sam.

That's plot movement.

Sometimes a storyline can bog down; it runs out of gas because there has been nothing to stimulate it. Plots *need* stimulus, they need to be pushed and prodded. Imagine a mystery-suspense story where the major character spends his days searching for clues and information. Imagine further that his search never seems to come any closer to what he is seeking, that his elusive prize remains well outside his grasp. Eventually, readers will tire of it, they'll become bored because nothing new seems to happen.

This is a plot bogged down. And even the most entertaining dialogue might not save it.

How do we avoid bogging down a plot? One way is to vary the pace of the story. If it's a mystery-suspense tale, then we should have the protagonist's interest in resolving things become less and less or greater and greater—either will do—and this will keep the reader's attention.

Another method would have external events take place that vary the intensity of the protagonist's interest in resolving things. For example, something can happen to the protagonist (he can almost be killed or taken prisoner or injured) and this can complicate his urge to resolve matters. The point is that these external events also push the plot along; they add variety to the pace and they keep the plot from bogging down.

See how Martin Cruz Smith does it in his novel, *Gorky Park*. We have three unexplained homicides found frozen in the snow, and the Russian investigator, Arkady Renko, begins a long trail to resolve things. Along the way two of his best men are killed, and he is impeded by the KGB. He senses that an American may be behind these murders, but he receives little support from his superiors. Finally, he seeks out the state prosecutor and indicates he wants to leave the case. At this point the search has yielded some information, but things have not moved much ahead, and without something else the plot could bog down. Note how things change rapidly in the following passage:

"Why do you care whether I stay on this case?" Arkady joined him.

"Histrionics aside, you're the best homicide investigator I have. It's my duty to keep you on the case." Iamskoy was friendly again.

"If the killer in Gorky Park was this American—"

"Bring me the evidence, and we will write the order for arrest together," Iamskoy said generously.

"If it was this American, I only have nine days. He leaves May Day Eve."

"Maybe you made more progress than you know."

"Nine days. I'll never get him."

"Do whatever you see fit, Investigator. You have great talents..."

What's happening here is that Smith is reinforcing the story direction. Unless something happened to push the investigation along, there would have been danger of plot bogdown. But Smith has the prosecutor give Arkady a verbal pat on the back. The investigation is recharged and the plot itself builds up steam.

The key to reinforcing the story direction is to bring something new, some new fact or feeling that must be faced. For Arkady the new fact was the prosecutor's strengthened support, and this, then, provides the motivation for Arkady to continue the investigation. The introduction of something new is a technique that can be used in a variety of situations.

- A love affair is dying. Should it be rekindled?
- A businessman has single-minded ambition. Should it be deflected?
- A shipboard cruise seems interminable. Should it be interrupted?

Something new. The instant cure for plot bogdown. *What's happening?* will get a shot in the arm.

Another example of this can be found in Margaret Atwood's story of life in a monotheocratic society, *The Handmaid's Tale*.

It is set sometime in the future, after the United States has been taken over by a sharp-eyed, stern-visaged army of religious fundamentalists. Women are relegated to reproductive functions, and their worth is directly proportional to how they produce. Certain younger women are trained as handmaids and assigned to households where they service the male in charge. Offred, the heroine, has not been able to conceive, and she worries that soon she will be dropped to "unwoman" status and exiled. She is at the doctor's, undergoing her regular monthly physical examination:

> "I could help you," he says. Whispers.
>
> "What?" I say.
>
> "Shhh," he says. "I could help you. I've helped others."
>
> "Help me?" I say, my voice as low as his. "How?" Does he know something, has he seen Luke, has he found, can he bring back?
>
> "How do you think?" he says, still barely breathing it. Is that his hand, sliding up my leg? He's taken off the glove. "This door's locked. No one will come in. They'll never know it isn't his."
>
> He lifts the sheet. The lower part of his face is covered by the white gauze mask, regulation. Two brown eyes, a nose, a head with brown hair on it. His hand in between my legs. "Most of these old guys can't make it anymore," he says. "Or they're sterile . . ."

Here again, something new has been injected. Until this moment Offred has no salvation from her inability to conceive. But in one conversation she has been offered a chance to confirm herself as a valuable member of the new society, and in the process we see the story take on added substance. Now there are alternatives for Offred, and she must grapple with a decision she didn't have to consider before the conversation.

In *Gorky Park*, Arkady is given new energy by the prosecutor's unexpected support; in *The Handmaid's Tale*,

Offred is given a choice she didn't have before. In both cases the stories become more interesting because the authors have relieved the unwavering path the characters were on. And dialogue is the technique both authors chose to use.

Lest we forget...isn't this another application of Trollope's reminder: *dialogue should contribute to the telling of the story?*

As we explore how dialogue can move a plot along, we should remember that dialogue is, itself, a technique for accomplishing the same purpose. Plot can certainly be pushed along by narrative; the story can be told in straightforward form, one sentence falling after the next, without any dialogue passages. But as we've seen, one healthy purpose of dialogue is to give immediacy to circumstances (when we portray conversation, it's happening *then*, *there*, *now*!), and to paint a dramatic picture. Dialogue can do it as a change of pace in the stream of narration, or it can do it as the essential story-telling mechanism. (For example, see the work of Ivy Compton Burnett or George Higgins—dialogue not only predominates, it is, by and large, the only form used.)

Dialogue, then, is a tool, and to be effective it must accomplish some purpose. As we've seen, it can highlight new circumstances, and it can do it in a way that will breathe new life into the story. Each passage of dialogue must do something to justify its use, otherwise it has no business in the story. William Sloane said it well some years ago:

"One common error with new writers is static dialogue. Writers guilty of this fault are aware that people talk, so they invent characters that talk, too. But these characters are dull talkers. They do not say anything. They do not talk to the point of the book..."

Which of the following moves the plot?

"Yes, I agree it's been a lovely day..."

or

"I did something today I've never done before."

The second passage introduces a new thought or circumstance. It is not static dialogue. From this we mold the dialogue to accomplish other purposes. Questions and answers could be used:

> "You see that lovely swan in the park lake?"
> "The kids chased it off."
> "You stopped them, didn't you?"
> "Your Rosie was at the front of the line..."

New facts and circumstances are introduced, and the plot doesn't have a chance to bog down.

Another technique is to have the characters discuss a third character (not present) and to plan something in relation to that third character. The plan itself will divulge new facts and circumstances. It will add depth to the plot. Take a look at the way John O'Hara does this in his novel *Ten North Frederick*. This is the story of a family in a small Pennsylvania town. They have lived in the same house for two generations, and O'Hara is relating a discussion between Charlotte, the mistress of the house, and a friend, both of whose sons were sent home from a birthday party because they misbehaved. The two women feel their sons were treated unfairly, and they plot retaliation, looking for ways to punish Blanche Montgomery, the mother who sent their boys home. Charlotte has an idea:

> "Well, the organized things, like the sewing club and the Altar Guild, one can't do anything about them. But there are other things that aren't organizations. There's that group you're getting together for next year, the little dinner club."
> "Arthur's chairman."
> "So Ben told me. Naturally, in my condition we had to decline, but so far you haven't even got a name for it, have you?"
> "No, we haven't even got a name for it so far. It's just an informal little dinner club. Once a month, November, December, January, February, March."
> "Just the sort of thing Blanche Montgomery's dying to

get in. An upstart from Reading and some nice people that have lived all their lives here won't even know about the club. After the way she's treated our children, I know I wouldn't enjoy sitting down to dinner with her. Well, I think that would do it for a start.''

"Oh, I can see to it they don't get an invitation..."

In talking about Blanche Montgomery the two women not only reveal their own characters, they move the story along. Up to the moment of this passage of dialogue, the existence of the dinner club has not been mentioned. Now, not only do we have Charlotte and her friend bringing it into the story, but using it, as well, as a strap to beat Blanche Montgomery with. From this bit of new information we find the plot moving.

- The dinner club will be by invitation only.
- It will be prestigious.
- Blanche Montgomery will not get an invitation.
- Blanche Montgomery will never become Charlotte's friend.
- Charlotte can veto any social aspirations Blanche Montgomery may have.

Doesn't this give the plot some substance? Now we know that whenever Charlotte does an unkind thing to Blanche Montgomery, the reason is clear. We also know that, because of her feelings, Charlotte definitely could do an unkind thing to Blanche, if the occasion demands it, at some point in the future. We anticipate, we wonder what might happen later, knowing that Charlotte has the motivation. This anticipation, as well as the actual events, continues to move the plot along.

What's happening?

Dialogue has taken us to a point in the story where we hadn't been moments before. That's plot movement.

And that's good writing.

5

Fiction or Fact?

Fact: something that has actual existence, an actual occurrence...

Fiction: something invented by the imagination or feigned, an invented story...

An actual occurrence.

An invented story.

Two separate items, according to Webster. After all, if something is factual, how can it be fictional?

If it's imagined, how can it have existed?

The two categories of story-writing, kept apart by the impenetrable wall of reality. We understand the differences, and we give credence to the distinctions. Writing about facts is what we've come to call nonfiction writing, and we know the kinds of writing it covers:

- journalism;
- how-to books;
- biography and autobiography;
- academic treatises;
- reference works.

The list could go on much longer, but the point is that what is nonfiction represents a wide body of work approximating eighty to ninety per cent of all publishing in any one year. The nonfiction writer is not the stepchild of the writing profession, as might have been the case a couple of generations ago. Nonfiction writing has developed its own products, and what we see today is an art form every bit as demanding as fiction, yet designed for different purposes.

Where fiction must create drama, nonfiction can report it; where fiction must develop character and plot, nonfiction has them at its fingertips.

But what of dialogue? Are the rules the same for fiction and nonfiction?

The answer has to be yes and no. Obviously, if we're reporting an event, and we quote someone at the scene, the quotation has to be accurate. We can't make it up, because that would turn it into fiction.

The same is true with biographies or real-life profiles. If we put strange words in the mouths of the people who appear on the page, there's bound to be someone who will say, "He (or she) never said that!" or "That's not the way I remember it being said." Fictionalizing dialogue in a biography will certainly affect its credibility and impact.

But what if we carve the dialogue around the edges, keeping its essential veracity, to make it dramatic?

Ah, that's when things get interesting. Because during the past twenty-five years or so, the lines between fiction and nonfiction have been getting blurred. In all seriousness, Tom Wolfe, the journalist, could say about his book, *The Right Stuff*:

> Goddamnit, I've got to think of ways to get people reading, to create an atmosphere right away that would absorb them. I just had to grab them by the lapels—and just hold them there...So I started developing a style that could capture the spontaneity of thought, not just speech...

Into the characters' heads he went, letting us know what they thought, their reactions and counter-reactions, what they wanted to say and to whom. It was dialogue, yet it wasn't, but it surely sounded as if someone might be talking!

The scene is the introduction of the seven Mercury astronauts to the press in 1959. Things go along in understated fashion until a reporter asks what the wives and children might have said about husbands and fathers as part of the space program. John Glenn starts to speak about how much he is supported by his wife and children, and then Tom Wolfe, the author, interrupts:

> What the hell was he talking about? *I don't think any of us could really go on something like this...What* possible difference could a *wife's attitude* make about an opportunity for a giant step up the great ziggurat? What was with this guy? It kept on in that fashion...

Is this one of the other astronauts thinking, is it a member of the press crew, is it, perhaps, one of the NASA people? Wolfe doesn't make any identification, but the impact of the words is clear. John Glenn's squeaky-clean approach to Mom, Country, and apple pie doesn't sit well with some of those in attendance.

Now, in the strictest sense, this isn't dialogue. But it isn't true narration, either. It's something else, more like an author's aside but seeming to reflect words that are on the tips of more than one tongue.

Wolfe is a careful author, and he wouldn't fabricate dialogue or twist it inside out just for dramatic value. But as he mentioned, he wanted to capture the spontaneity of thought, he wanted to grab his audience by its lapels. Since he was dealing with nonfiction, his approaches were limited, and he used thought processes as a way of developing immediacy and drama.

No, it's not dialogue, but it's probably as close as a nonfiction writer will get when he can't use the actual words someone says or the actual thought processes someone has.

But suppose a writer wants to use dialogue, even though he or she is dealing with a factual issue? Suppose, further, the writer doesn't have the exact words available, only the general sequence of events. Putting words in the mouths of characters is a literary no-no, and I've seen otherwise stalwart books ripped apart by critics because of the license the author took.

It's one thing, of course, if we're dealing with history, and we wish to take dramatic license with some well-known figure... George Washington, for instance, or Marco Polo or a well-remembered Roman Emperor. The reader knows the author is taking dramatic license and makes allowance, especially when that historical figure is only one of numerous characters in the story. In fact, introducing real-life characters into a work of fiction is an often-used tactic, but the reader knows, and the author knows the reader knows, that dramatic license is being taken.

It's another thing, though, when the major characters in a work of nonfiction have words put into their mouths. How can the reader assume the authenticity of what is written?

He can't, unless...

Unless the author lays his cards on the table. Unless the author makes the reader his partner in the progress of the work.

We are going to write this a different way, the author can say. I want this to be nonfiction, but I want to use fabricated dialogue, too. Go along with me, trust me, I will give you truth.

These, then, are the seeds of what has become known as the "nonfiction novel," a type of work that is a faithful representation of fact but uses fictional techniques to tell the story.

Truman Capote is credited with devising the form, and he presented it for the first time in his story of the multiple murders of the Clutter family in 1959 in Kansas, *In Cold Blood*. His decision to write a book like this

> ...was based on a theory I've harbored since I first began writing professionally...it seemed to me that journalism, reportage, could be forced to yield a serious new art form: the "non fiction" novel...It is imaginative, narrative reporting...

Capote's eyes were those of the reporter, but his instincts were those of the fiction writer, and so his work follows the events closely, from the moment the murder scheme is hatched, through its execution, the flight of the killers, their eventual capture and confessions, their trials and their executions. The way he presents his story, however, is far removed from straight reportage. Instead of chronological progression and unbroken narration, he uses techniques such as flashbacks, foreshadowing, intercutting of different story strands—just as any fiction writer would do.

And he uses dialogue. But the question is—the dialogue of the fiction writer or the reporter?

In a key scene in the book, the two killers have been captured and are being taken in separate cars back to the town where the crime occurred. Dick, one of the killers, has confessed, but Perry, the other, has denied any involvement. The police try to prod Perry by telling him about Dick's confession, but to no avail. Then one of the detectives mentions an incident some years before when Perry is supposed to have beaten a black man to death. Perry gasps...

> ...He twists around in his seat until he can see, through the rear window, the motorcade's second car, see inside it. "The tough boy!" Turning back, he stares at the dark streak of desert highway. "I thought it was a stunt. I didn't believe you. That Dick let fly. The tough boy! Oh, a real brass boy. Wouldn't harm the fleas on a dog. Just ran over the dog." He spits. "I never killed any nigger. But *he* thought so. I always knew if we ever got caught, if Dick ever really let fly, dropped his guts all over the goddam floor—I knew he'd tell about the nigger." He spits again. "So Dick was afraid of me? That's amusing. I'm very amused. What he don't know is, I almost did shoot him."

Capote could not possibly have gotten this quotation directly from the policemen in the car (in fact, at the subsequent trial, the policemen give their recollections of the conversation, and these barely touch on what Capote has Perry say). Capote had to have manufactured this dialogue, at least sufficiently to provide it with drama.

There are, of course, many other examples of recast dialogue in the book. But Capote had no reason to hang his head. By calling the book a "nonfiction" novel, he permitted himself the freedom to turn his dialogue into more than simple, realistic recounting.

He gave it substance, and he gave it immediacy.

Is it a fact, then? Of course it is.

But it is not strict journalism. The events Capote describes actually took place; the words the people say may or may not have been uttered.

Capote warns us in the beginning. It is to be a "nonfiction" novel, and from this we should know there will be license taken.

Dialogue, thus, need not be limited to reportorial accuracy. It can blossom to develop character, move the plot along, set a mood . . . as long as the general sense of what a character is supposed to have said is maintained.

In the example given, Capote knew Perry had reacted sardonically when told of Dick's confession. Capote kept Perry in character with the dialogue; he didn't stray far from what he had been told about Perry's actual reaction.

And in this sense he retained a certain journalistic integrity. One can fabricate dialogue in a nonfiction novel, but the closer to what was actually said, the better. The dramatic license for the nonfiction novel, therefore, is limited to purpose and consequence . . . *this is what I want to use it for . . . this is what I want it to accomplish . . .*

Several years after Capote's book, Norman Mailer came along with *his* "nonfiction" novel, *The Executioner's Song*. Here again we see the same dilemma with respect to how much to dramatize and how much to keep in its unadorned state. Mailer, though, felt at ease with substantial use of dialogue. In this story of the last nine months of the life of murderer Gary Gilmore, Mailer researched extensively, claiming to have interviewed well over one hundred people and to have examined a variety of documents. Like Truman Capote, Mailer states that his book is a true-life story, based on fact. He indicates, however, that the facts we're going to get may not be without some question:

> This book does its best to be a factual account of the activities of Gary Gilmore from April 9th, 1976...until his execution a little more than nine months later...this does not mean it has come a great deal closer to the truth than the recollections of witnesses...

Mailer does not claim, nor did Capote, that their books were journalistic reproductions of events and statements. Mailer says his book *does its best* and, as with Capote, we have to take him at his word.

So, Mailer can feel free to write of Gary Gilmore's conversation with his cousin, Brenda, after he tries to shoplift a tape deck, is stopped by a security guard, flees in his girl friend's car, then leaves it in a parking lot where it is impounded by the police:

> He had it figured out. "You explain to the police that Nicole had nothing to do with it. That way, they'll let her have the car back."
>
> "You're a man," Brenda said. "Go down and get the car back yourself."
>
> "You won't help me?"
>
> "I'll help you write a confession. I'll see it's delivered."
>
> "Brenda, there's a lot of loudspeakers in the back of the car. I ripped them off in a drive-in movie."
>
> "How many?"
>
> "Five or six."
>
> "Just to be doing something," said Brenda. "Like a little kid."
>
> Gary nodded. There was the sorrow in his eyes of knowing he would never see Canada...

How much of this did the participants actually remember? Do people remember conversations this way?

Perhaps the best question is: does it really matter, if we're writing a nonfiction novel?

Norman Mailer, however, does more with *The Executioner's Song* than just relay dialogue. He also characterizes that dialogue, and in this way he has taken a step beyond Capote.

Note above that Mailer has Gilmore with sorrow in his eyes because he'll never see Canada. Clearly, this is fiction technique, a way of adding dimension to what is said. Mailer does this over and over in the book:

- *Gary looked disappointed*, "This is one movie," he told her, "I want to see again."
- Gary said he hated to watch TV. He especially hated the police shows. *Nicole yawned.*
- *He gave a turn to his mouth that was almost a smile.* "You know," he said...

Mailer embellishes his dialogue with gestures, habits, and manners, and the same questions apply: how does he know, and do his interviews reveal these circumstances?

Or, because he has called this a "nonfiction" novel, is there really no problem?

If this were straight journalism, or a how-to book or a biography, such characterizations of dialogue would be omitted, unless the author could point to some source for evidence. Even then there might be some raised eyebrows because we're relying on someone else's subjective judgment to provide a word picture each of us can grasp.

That is, if I tell an interviewer one of the characters had an angry look when something was said, can we assume I am correct? Perhaps the angry look was because of a sudden toothache ...or an unhappy memory not related to the action on the page. The point is, my subjective judgment could influence the dialogue and the action that follows it...and I could be incorrect!

The fiction writer has it much easier—he or she knows what

the dialogue characterizations mean and can manipulate the character to respond properly. If the fiction writer describes the appearance of a flush on a character's neck, the chances are it's in relation to heightened emotions:

> "I-I don't know what to say..." she murmured, a rose hue blossoming along her neck...

But if it's nonfiction, that flush could be from any number of causes, and it may have little to do with the storyline. The nonfiction writer can make only an educated guess, unless he has specific information from someone who knows.

The object lesson? Be careful characterizing dialogue when writing nonfiction.

And make sure whatever dialogue characterizations are used follow the words of Anthony Trollope: they must *contribute to the telling of the story*.

6

Dialogue's Many Faces

Some years ago the word got around that I was writing—and selling— erotic fiction. It was true, though I didn't beat my breast over it. I used pen names, and I didn't let it interfere with other writing projects.

One day a friend sought me out. "Why," she asked, "do you write that stuff? It's trash."

Trash?

"I enjoy doing it," I answered.

"There are so many other things you could write."

"I'm pretty good at it," I offered.

Trash?

"It just isn't...literature," she tried to explain.

"I get an occasional fan letter."

"Hah! Bad taste is catching..."

The old axiom sprang to my mind...*one person's trash, another person's treasure*...

"The point," I said, "is to tell a good story. It doesn't matter what you call it."

Trash or treasure, erotic stories can tell a good story. They provide enjoyment and escape.

For most readers that's enough.

Enjoyment and escape are the twin supports for a type of writing called "genre" or "category" or "formula" fiction. The words mean, simply, that stories are standardized to conform to certain preconceived patterns. There are rules to the game of writing these stories, and they should be followed.

We've heard (and probably read) many of the categories: mystery, suspense, romance, gothic, western, horror, erotic. The plots within each category are similar to one another, the characterizations straightforward, and the settings appropriate to the atmosphere the author wishes to achieve. Thus a romance might be set in the lushness of the Caribbean, and a mystery might be set in the remoteness of an Alaskan mining camp.

But the stories can be category fiction.

And the dialogue must support this.

That is, the dialogue must not do more than contribute to what the category fiction is designed to do.

Consider the western-fiction category. The cowboy and his horse and his gun and the outlaws...

> Action, action, action is the thing. So long as you keep your hero jumping through fiery hoops on every page you're all right...There has to be a woman, but not much of one. A good horse is much more important...

Max Brand wrote that some time ago, and he meant it to apply to writing for the pulps. But it still has relevance today. Which of the following would be more appropriate to current western fiction?

> "Your eyes sparkle with the dust of starlight, your beauty overwhelms me."
> "Oh Gregor, it's these lovely Montana evenings..."
> > *or*
> "There's a roundness to you that's exciting."
> "Hmmm," she smiled, "I guess that's a compliment..."

Certainly, the second passage is something even the most

stereotypical western character would feel comfortable saying. It's simple and direct, and it carries the implication of much more. If the woman excites him because she's round, that implies a burgeoning sexuality, and that, of course, opens the door to further imaginings.

But the dialogue in the first passage is not something we would expect a westerner to say—especially the man. It's too poetic, too image-conveying. This doesn't mean, of course, that the western character can't do all of this and more; rather it means that in western-category fiction, such dialogue seems out of place.

The point, then, is simply this: dialogue must conform to the demands of the fiction category being presented. We can't have an erotic story dwell on the safest manner of tethering a horse, any more than we can have a mystery story over-concern itself with whether John loves Mary or Mary loves John, as the romance category requires.

We might call this "standardization" of the technique of writing dialogue because it means that the dialogue must fit a pattern. If it's a western...if it's erotic...if it's suspense... and so forth.

See how Leslie Marmon Silko standardizes the dialogue in *Yellow Woman*, a western-category story of an Indian, Silva, who comes upon a woman at the river bank. He claims to be a *ka'tsina* spirit and names her Yellow Woman. He leads her off to spend the night—two nights—with him somewhere on the Indian reservation. Silva admits that he rustles cattle, and one morning he is gone, returning after a few hours with fresh meat which he washes and strips in order to sell. Throughout the story there are references to the legends of the *ka'tsina* spirit and Yellow Woman, but nothing further is spelled out. Silva and the woman ride towards Marquez, Mexico to sell the meat, which Silva has strapped on the woman's horse. They meet a white rancher on the trail:

      "Where did you get the fresh meat?" the white man asked.

"I've been hunting," Silva said, and when he shifted his weight in the saddle the leather creaked.

"The hell you have, Indian. You've been rustling cattle. We've been looking for the thief a long time."

The rancher was fat and sweat began to soak through his white cowboy shirt and the wet cloth stuck to the thick rolls of belly fat. He almost seemed to be panting from the exertion of talking, and he smelled rancid, maybe because Silva scared him.

Silva turned and smiled. "Go back up the mountain, Yellow Woman."

The white man got angry when he heard Silva speak a language he couldn't understand. "Don't try anything, Indian. Just keep riding to Marquez. We'll call the state police from there"...

Note the elements of standardization here: the white man calls Silva *Indian*, showing barely-concealed contempt and disdain. There's an automatic jump to the conclusion that Silva must be a cattle rustler (because he's on a horse and carrying fresh meat). Note, too, that Silva and the woman converse in their own language, thus alienating the white man and at the same time emphasizing the gulf between the two cultures.

These are the basics of western-category fiction, and the dialogue must not seem out of place. Suppose, for example, the cowboy had ridden up and said, "Hi there! My name's Tex Cody. Mighty nice day for a ride." And Silva, instead of projecting menace, had said, "I've heard of you. Run the big spread over yonder, right?"

Such cliché-western dialogue would hardly fit the occasion of the story. But Silko kept the dialogue within the characterizations, the white man contemptuous of Silva and Silva contemptuous of the white man.

What if it's an erotic story we're going to write? Is the dialogue capable of being standardized?

Of course it is.

But be sure we understand...erotic is *not* pornographic, it is not the writing of sexually explicit material for the sole purpose of portraying sexual conduct. Erotic literature uses sexually explicit material, but only in furtherance of an underlying story. It is not sex for the sake of sex.

Anthony Burgess gives us a good yardstick:

> A pornographic work represents social acts of sex, frequently of a perverse or wholly fantastic nature, often without consulting the limits of physical possibility. Such works encourage solitary fantasy...The book is, in a sense, a substitute for a sexual partner...

Now, the following would be appropriate dialogue for an erotic story:

> "Do you like it this way?" he whispered.
>
> "Oh yes. I never knew it could be like this," she said.
>
> "You really think I'm that good?"
>
> "Marvelous. The best."
>
> "Honest? You really mean it?"
>
> "Marvelous," she groaned. "One of the two best sexual experiences I've had in my entire life. Ouch! What are you doing?"
>
> "Who was the other?"

This is from Dan Greenberg's story, *Was it Good For You, Too?* It is satire, and the man and woman are in a sexual experiment with wires attached to their bodies and a covey of doctors observing them. They had never met before the experiment, and suddenly, intimacy grows.

Jealousy, too. Which dooms the experiment. The underlying theme is clear, of course—it is the bizarre nature of the experiment. But note the dialogue: intimate, highly emotional, pleasure-producing, and sexually explicit.

All of which is standard fare for erotic fiction. Greenberg doesn't have his characters use four-letter words, he doesn't have them pant or scream, he doesn't have them resort to jungle conduct.

Erotic stories should be pleasurable without being demeaning, and the dialogue must abide by this standard.

Yet, writing category fiction means more than keeping the dialogue standardized. The style of the writing itself must be considered. Category fiction does not encourage what we might call a high-flown literary style (style, in other words, that is complicated, multi-dimensional, almost analytical). Dialogue which attempts to prove something or which says one thing but means something else or which does not try to involve the reader has no place in category fiction. In basic terms, dialogue in category fiction must:

- be simple;
- be emotionally charged;
- encourage reader involvement;
- emphasize action.

In a suspense story, if a character is running for his life, we ought to feel his fear:

> "I-I'm not sure," he said, gulping for breath. "Every exit's blocked . . ."

The line of dialogue means what it says. It's simple, direct, uncomplicated. If the prior passages have been done properly, we, the readers, have been pulled along with the rising tension; we've entered the struggle too, and now we, also, face the character's dilemma.

We've become involved in the emotion and the action. Category fiction demands this involvement, and clean, simple dialogue that stresses emotion and action is the best way to achieve it.

See how Robert Ludlum does it in *The Aquitaine Progression*. This is the story of an American lawyer, Joel Converse, who stumbles on a global political conspiracy while in Geneva, Switzerland. Converse has made contact with General Bertholdier, a retired French army officer, hoping to gain further information. He tells Bertholdier he has traced foreign arms shipments from the United States to various foreign destinations.

Bertholdier's eyes were fixed, controlled. "I would know nothing about such things, of course," he said.

"Of course," agreed Converse. "But the fact that my client does—through me—and the additional fact that neither he nor I have any desire whatsoever to call attention to them must tell you something."

"Frankly, not a thing."

"Please, General. One of the first principles of free enterprise is to cripple your competition, step in and fill the void."

The soldier drank, gripping the glass firmly. He lowered it and spoke. "Why did you come to me?"

"Because you were there."

"What!"

There's nothing complicated in this passage. Ludlum has created tension between his characters, he has emotion and the promise of action spilling out. Note the suspense techniques here: Converse knows something Bertholdier does not know. We—the readers—know that Converse knows. The suspense is in wondering when—or if—Converse will let Bertholdier in on it.

Converse toys with him briefly, and the suspense grows higher. Will he or won't he...?

Then he does tell him, and the result is an explosive reaction.

Clearly, Ludlum, in this passage, has followed the basics of category-fiction writing... the writing is simple and emotionally charged, it encourages reader involvement through Converse's struggle to find answers, and it emphasizes action.

But suspense stories are not the only vehicles in which these items should flourish. Other fiction categories use them, as well. Mystery stories, for instance.

There *is* a difference between suspense and mystery stories. We should be aware of that. In mystery stories there usually is a puzzle—often a crime—that must be solved, and the lead character is a detective or some other determined individual with a mission to find the solution. In suspense stories, the lead character is often caught up in the action, and whatever solution he or she creates is to extricate himself or herself from further danger. In the parlance of another time, characters in suspense stories are part of the problem, characters in mystery stories are part of the solution.

Eleanor Sullivan puts it succinctly:

> A detective story is objective. A suspense story, on the other hand, is subjective, and is more often than not a study in some depth of the dark side of human nature...
> In suspense the reader can know things that major characters don't...

On the mystery scene, there is scarcely a better known writer than John MacDonald. His Travis McGee novels have sold millions of copies, and when MacDonald puts one together, the pieces slide firmly into place.

Travis McGee stories are mystery stories (though an argument could be made that they also contain elements of the suspense genre). MacDonald does not deviate from the basic rules of dialogue; he doesn't pretend to be writing anything more high-flown than a readable, workman-like mystery.

He knows his audience, and he knows what it wants.

In *The Lonely Silver Rain*, he has McGee search for a stolen yacht which he believes to be stashed somewhere in the Florida Keys. McGee hires his friend Mick, a pilot, to do some flyovers, and Mick is able to locate the yacht, hidden in dense brush. McGee goes to the yacht, where he finds three dead bodies. But he notifies the owners, and is rewarded with a substantial amount of cash. He has just handed Mick twenty thousand dollars:

> "Hoo weee!" he said. "Makes my teeth hurt."
> "Some well-dressed little Latin types came to my client to find out who found the boat."
> "Nobody has come to me."
> "They might."

"What boat is that?"

"I can't remember, either."

"Wonder who wasted those kids," he said, frowning.

"What kids?"

"Okay, okay, okay," he said. "You get real cautious, don't you?"

"And I'm walking around, talking and everything..."

MacDonald touches each of the elements we need for good category-fiction writing. His dialogue is simple and emotionally charged—McGee and Mick discuss the fact someone is looking into who found the hidden yacht, and the menace of all that seethes from their talk. They do not want to be tied into the matter at all, and this serves to heighten the tension. The fact that both men are concerned for their safety gives us a lever by which to reach out for reader identification. (It's a classic situation—innocent men targeted for something unpleasant even though they have done nothing wrong.) We *feel* for the unfairness of their predicament.

And then, of course, their conspiracy of silence emphasizes how they hope to avoid the unpleasantness. It isn't action, really, except in the negative sense, but what is underscored here is the fact that they must avoid a confrontation with the "little Latin types" who are looking for them.

It's the menace of being discovered, and to avoid this there will certainly be action.

Mystery, suspense, erotic, western...these stories all move across the same field, representing yardsticks and boundaries and content to provide a good story. Romance writing, also, falls into this area, and once again the same principles apply.

Is there any difference when we write:

"There's no helping me...I'm in love with you..."

"Please, Carrie, please, I-I can't offer anything..."

than when we write:

"Someone's asking questions about us."

"Out the back way. Quickly!..."

The first passage is in the romance category, and it hits the elements we've outlined for this type of fiction. The dialogue must draw emotion out of the characters, and in the process draw empathy from the readers. Romance stories demand wide-ranging emotions, and the hope is that these emotions will also be felt by the readers.

Reader identification, simple, emotionally charged, and holding the promise of action.

Note the second passage. This could work in suspense or mystery stories and meet the same tests as does the romance passage. Without more dialogue it might also appear in other forms of category fiction, because it sketches a predicament that could be present in all of them.

That's the point, really. Category-fiction writing, or major portions of it, can be interchangeable. The same passage of dialogue in a romance, for instance, can also appear in a western. Another passage might serve an erotic story as well as it could advance a suspense story.

It means simply this: if we learn how to write for one category, we can write for another.

But don't forget: dialogue writing that doesn't fit the category is like a thickly iced, moist, rich cake...

In which the cook forgot the sugar.

Part B

The Details of Dialogue

Prelude

An important aspect of dialogue writing is to cope with the little situations, the details that can cause a perfectly well-planned passage to appear stilted. We know that the Master Key situations address the foundations of good dialogue writing, and that these foundations must be sturdy enough to support a story well told with deft characterizations, believable plot, and admirable settings. The Master Keys tell us how the essentials of good dialogue writing contribute to—in fact, control—the progress of a story, but they don't provide the more highly calibrated techniques that can bring about the snuggest fit between dialogue and story structure.

For this we must narrow our focus, moving away from the broad perspective of dialogue that furthers characterization, for example, and catch up with dialogue techniques that do less substantial—though no less important—things. I call these the details of dialogue because we are dealing with items that can't influence an entire dialogue passage yet will influence a line or even a phrase of dialogue.

The details of dialogue are important precisely for this reason. Each tiny step we take to improve our dialogue writing—even to changing "he says" to "he exclaims," for example—has the effect of channelling our attention to the individual words we are using. And it is those individual words that make up the ultimate product we offer as writers.

So we start with details, and we begin to understand that a dialogue passage isn't a jumble of words placed on the page because it *feels* good. There must be reasons why those words in that order, modified by still other words, are there. We ask ourselves some important questions:

- does it fit the mood of the story?
- are we being consistent?
- can—or should—we do without?
- is there something else more appropriate?
- will the reader be confused?

The details of dialogue have to be addressed if we want to answer questions like these properly. Take the matter of gesturing as a companion to a dialogue passage, for example. If we want to highlight a particular emotion, we might use a physical gesture to buttress a passage of dialogue like this:

"I'm damned if I'll make any more excuses for you!" he said, slamming his fist on the desk...

Or if we want to make the gesture less combative:

He tapped the pencil against his pinky ring. "I'm damned if I'll make any more excuses for you," he said, softly...

This is a detail of dialogue. It does not affect the general mood of an entire passage, nor does it try to move the story ahead to any degree. Yet a detail such as this—whether to gesture and how to do it—will create an image in the reader's mind, even if for only an instant, and that image, along with all the others we have established, will combine to produce a portrait of a character or a place or an event that forms the backbone of the story.

There are, of course, many more details of dialogue in the

following section than there were Master Keys, and this is as it should be. The Master Keys are more general, more encompassing, and, after all, there are only so many pillars needed to make a foundation. But the details of dialogue are really endless. Each of us can develop a list that can touch on items unthought of just days before. But in the following chapters I have tried to cull those details that seem to arise most frequently because, after all, the point of this book is to get on with the business of writing dialogue. I—we—should not be tempted to search out the most esoteric elements of dialogue production just so we can say we have touched every base.

The point is that in the fourteen chapters to follow, the bases are covered, and what is there will serve the writer well.

These details of dialogue are mirrored in literature through the ages, and as we go over them their relevance will become obvious.

7

Do I Show, Do I Tell?

In Vladimir Nabokov's novel, *Lolita*, a character rushes in with the words:

> "Mrs. Humbert, sir, has been run over and you'd better come quick."

To the protagonist, Humbert Humbert, this is news with a joyful twist; now he can have his young stepdaughter to himself, now he can shuck the pretense of the dutiful husband.

It is this event which allows Humbert to begin a cross-country sexual odyssey with his nymphet, Lolita. A key passage and a key transition.

Note that Nabokov accomplishes all of this with one simple sentence of dialogue. He could, of course, have described Mrs. Humbert's death, and the plot itself would not have been affected. Mrs. Humbert would still die, and Humbert would still go on his sexual odyssey.

But Nabokov chose dialogue instead of narration, and somehow it seems proper.

The key thing with dialogue is its immediacy. What is being said is happening *now*; what the characters talk about is occurring *now*! In the passage above, Humbert is conversing with others when the news of his wife's accident is brought. The immediacy of the news is underscored by the abrupt change in the conversational pattern it produces. Think of it. . . we're discussing a new book or someone's latest allergy when the word flashes: your spouse has met with an accident!

The immediacy of the news is apparent—it has just happened *now, this minute*!

Narration doesn't accomplish this sort of thing as well. It takes a longer-range view of events, more concerned with the fullness of description than with the rush of instant action. Narration gives us a tool to paint time and space in broader perspectives than does dialogue, yet both should work together.

Generally, dialogue is best used when we:
- wish to focus on a specific event and need the reactions of the participants;
- want to break up lengthy narrative passages, gain a change of pace;
- want to develop a shortcut to characterizations;
- wish to inject a sense of life into the scene.

Narrative, on the other hand, takes us further and can show us more. It is description and summary and scene-business rolled together. It is expository writing with the purpose of moving the story along. William Sloane gives us a pretty good handle on the elements of narration:

> Narration is not an easy thing to define. One way of getting at it is to say that it is all that part of a manuscript that answers three basic questions. What has happened? What is happening? What is going to happen?

If dialogue shows us immediacy, then narrative tells us what is happening.

Note how the two can work together. A.B. Guthrie uses elements of each in *The Way West*, his story of people pushing westward during the nineteenth century. The narrative portion describes the landscape, and the dialogue characterizes the speakers.

Lije whooed his oxen when he came to the top of the hill. Rebecca walked up to him and saw the train winding down and, below it, Fort Laramie, white as fresh wash, with trees waving and shade dark on the grass and the river fringed with woods. More to herself than to Lije she said, "I never thought to be so glad just to see a building."

"It's Fort Laramie. Sure."

"Not because it's a fort. Just because it's a building."

"It's Fort Laramie all the same."

"You reckon they've got chairs there, Lije? Real chairs?"

There was a light in his eyes. He said, "Sure," and cut a little caper with his feet and sang out:

"To the far-off Pacific sea,
  Will you go, will you go, old
  girl with me?"

She said, "I just want to sit in a chair..."

We learn much more about the surrounding terrain than about Lije and Rebecca through the narrative. We see the Fort and the river and hill and the woods. The narrative provides us, as it is supposed to, a sense of what is going on. In this case it is Lije and Rebecca cresting the hill and reaching their objective, Fort Laramie. It also tells us what the countryside is like and how Lije and Rebecca hope to fit in.

The dialogue shows us the relief the couple feel on reaching their objective, and it's obvious they are both tired. We should be able to *feel* their fatigue if the dialogue contains a sense of immediacy.

And the feel is there...Rebecca wants to sit in a chair. Haven't we all had that feeling at some time? Just a chair, any chair. A place to rest weary bones.

What Guthrie has done here is give us the broader picture with his narrative and then focus on the dialogue for close-ups of Lije and Rebecca. It is a classic use of the two techniques and, as we see, it works well.

Suppose we want to describe a street scene, and we want to establish an atmosphere of menace. We can do it either way:

> The shadows curved away and evaporated into blackness, vague lights muted the curb edges, and a fine dust seemed to hang in the air. Rough brick walls towered over them, following the shadows into the night, and the stillness was palpable...

or

> "It's too quiet," he said.
> "Who's walking the streets at 3 A.M., anyway?"
> "Wonder what's behind those brick walls."
> "C'mon, let's move it."
> "Wish we had a moon to go by."
> "Watch it! The curb..."
> "Why didn't we wait till it was light out for God's sake!"

Which of these two passages is more dramatic? Which provides the reader with a greater sense of immediacy, which is more alive? The chances are it's the dialogue passage. The conflict between the two characters and the environment is easily portrayed in just a few lines. For the narrative passage to work it would take more time and even then would we have the immediacy we seek?

This doesn't mean, of course, that a narrative passage can't paint a scene of conflict or menace—in fact, we have a good start on one right here. But what dialogue can accomplish with just a few lines might take narrative several paragraphs to do.

So we have to ask ourselves when we have the choice between narrative and dialogue—do we want it short and lively, or do we want it longer and more sedate?

The question hangs there for each of us.

Generally, though, dialogue and narrative work together, as a team. There's a place for each one in a piece of written work, and it is the writer's task to blend them well.

Consider change of pace. Narrative proceeds for a couple of

pages, then we inject some dialogue, then we go back to narrative. It can work in the reverse, of course...dialogue, then narrative, then dialogue...but it seems less important to break up the flow of dialogue than it does to break up the flow of narrative. What we seek to do is never allow the reader's attention to flag; we keep the pace of the written work ebbing and flowing so the reader must stay on top of things.

Dialogue as a change of pace works well. See how Judith Rossner does it with *Attachments*, her novel of a young woman, Nadine, who has a passionate crush on a pair of Siamese twins, Amos and Eddie. She conspires to live with them in California where they have a large house and pool. One day Nadine swims in the nude while they watch. Just before the dialogue passage below, there are two long narrative paragraphs describing how she slowly removes her clothes, tests the water, languidly dives in and swims a few laps. She climbs out, towels off in front of them, then drops to the grass...

"How do we go about this?" I asked.

"Tell us what you want us to do," Eddie asked.

"I want to get in between you," I told him.

Obligingly, they went back to their lying down, facing-each-other position. I climbed over Eddie's legs and inched up on my belly until my nose was touching their joint, which was closer to the ground than I'd hoped. Too close for me to crawl under.

"You're making this very difficult," I told the joint.

"Here, Eddie said. "Lie down over there." He pointed to the grass near their feet. Obediently I lay flat on my back on the grass, sexual desire temporarily smothered by anxiety. But it was too late to turn back. My heart beat wildly. They squirmed onto their knees.

"Now lie on your side," Eddie said...

Then, for the next two pages it's all narration. In almost four pages the only dialogue is what we have above. Rossner could have described everything without dialogue, but doesn't it make things more interesting if we have the characters doing some talking? We get glimpses of their character, and we can find ourselves identifying with them easily.

Rossner has changed the pace with her dialogue, breaking up a lengthy passage on the sexual antics of one neurotic woman and a pair of Siamese twins. The reader is bound to pay more attention when the characters are talking because it's interesting to see reactions and counter-reactions. Narrative can't really give us that.

But then dialogue can't give us the long-range view of events either. Dialogue is for close-ups, for immediacy, for breathing a sense of life into a scene.

Remember that, and the blend between dialogue and narrative will be smooth, indeed.

8

He Says...Or Does He?

I recall reading one of James Thurber's works dealing with reminiscences of Harold Ross, the highly praised, unpredictable, somewhat zany editor of *The New Yorker*. Ross and his editorial staff—espeically Wolcott Gibbs—developed some editorial rules for manuscripts, and that was that.

One of the rules, according to Thurber, was that a passage of dialogue is best followed by "said." Anything else—"shouts" or "exclaims" or "retorts," for example—is just wasted motion. No verb, in other words, should substitute for "said."

It got me thinking..."Stuff it in your ear!" he...*said*? Wouldn't "retort" be better?

Or..."My God!" he...*said*? It seemed to me "exclaimed" would fit more easily.

I thought further. The sense of Ross's rule began to dawn. A writer should be able to phrase dialogue so the impact of the words would be clear. "Go to Hell!" he shouted—could be a redundancy. "Go to Hell!" itself is a strongly worded statement, and why do we need "he shouted"?

Of course, maybe we don't need any modifying phrase at all. "Go to Hell!" could stand by itself. No "shout," no "said," no nothing. The reader's imagination could probably conjure a fitting modifier.

Today, even *The New Yorker* allows substitutions for "said." Yet the rule shouldn't be dismissed because what Ross and his editors were trying to accomplish had considerable merit. A writer *should* be able to create dialogue that doesn't rely on the descriptive modifier; the words a character speaks should carry the emotion in which the words are spoken:

> "You-you aren't my dead uncle's long-lost great-great grandson!"...

> "Oh Everett, I love these children so..."

In the first sentence do we need modifiers like *he gasped*, or *he blurted out*...? Wouldn't *he said* work as well? Perhaps we don't need to say anything—maybe that would work even better.

In the second sentence, do we need *she purred*, *she whispered*—? We could insert *she said*, and it wouldn't detract from the impact of the dialogue. Then, too, perhaps nothing at all would be even better.

There are no precise rules on when to use "he said," when to use a substitute, and when to use nothing. It's a matter of feel and an understanding that the reader doesn't want to be overwhelmed by a rush of descriptive modifiers. Generally, however, we can say this:

- "he/she said" is the basic modifier, and it should be used at least three-quarters of the time any modifier is used;
- a page of dialogue should not go by without a couple of "he/she saids";
- when in doubt, leave the "said" out—add nothing;
- in dialogue between two people, use "he/she said" with only one of the characters—nothing with the other.

In the cleanest writing, of course, we don't use anything at all. We let the dialogue passages stand for themselves. But if we have to use a descriptive modifier, the important thing to re-

member is that "he/she said" serves two purposes: it is an identification device (letting the reader know who is speaking and
what the speaker is feeling), and it can change the pace of the
dialogue, allowing the reader a slight respite from one unmodified dialogue passage after another. It can give breathing
room.

Dialogue without any "saids" is as close as we'll get to script
writing, and there are writers who feel that this is the art toward
which we should strive. "The more nearly a novel resembles a
play in prose form" wrote Lawrence Block some years ago, "the
simpler it is for the average reader to come to grips with it." I
think what he meant was that readers fasten on dialogue
passages, enabling themselves to gain a better understanding of
the story.

Note how Thomas McGuane develops a storyline without using any "said." In *Nobody's Angel* he has Patrick, his protagonist, meet up with his dead sister's lover, who happens to
be an Indian. They have never laid eyes on one another before:

"Do you need to see me?" Patrick asks.

"If there is something between us."

"What's that supposed to mean? Is that Indian talk?"

"I don't know."

"What's your name?"

"David Catches."

"Well, they're going to bury my sister. Will you be going?"

"You'll make another speech. I don't want to hear that
kind of thing."

"Then why don't you come to the house tonight?"...

Except for the first line, every passage is without modifier.
We know who is talking, don't we? The emotions of the
characters are clear from the words they use—we don't need any
help. This reads almost like a script.

Note one thing, however: McGuane uses a question-and-
answer technique, and this is one way of avoiding any "saids."

If we know the identity of the questioner, then we also know the identity of the responder (assuming there are only two people in the scene), and one of the reasons—that of identification—for using "he/she said" doesn't apply. Note, too, that the nature of the question-and-answer exchange tends to be conflict-producing, and so the tension between the two characters doesn't really need further depiction through descriptive modifiers.

But what if we don't feel comfortable unless we use "he/she said"? A lengthy passage without a "said" might not be to our liking:

> My rule is this: always use 'said' unless you must characterize the action further by telling *how* something is said...It is best to remember that *what* is said in any page of dialogue is at least three times as important as *how* it is said...

Marjorie Franco wrote that a while ago, and it still works. Suppose we want a character to show disagreement. He can say:

> "No! I won't buy that!"

But, suppose we want anger to be demonstrated, as well. Then we write:

> "No! I won't buy that!" *He slammed his fist on the table*...

The dialogue passage tells us what is said—that there is disagreement—and the modifier tells us how it is said—in anger.

> "I love you," he said, stroking the back of her neck. (Intimate.)
>
> "I love you," he confessed. (Vulnerable.)
>
> "I love you," he shouted. (Prideful.)

The words of each dialogue passage are the same, but the way the words are said differs. How the dialogue is uttered becomes important when we want to underline the dialogue words themselves.

Call it characterizing the dialogue, perhaps, and we wouldn't be far off. We are actually giving some personality to the dialogue. But there is more than one way to characterize the dialogue; we won't have to be limited to synonyms for the "saids." In the hands of an accomplished writer the personality of the dialogue can blossom through the use of interior monologue—that is, by having the actor think of the words he/she has just used and *characterize* them. The "saids" then take on added substance.

See how Eudora Welty does it with her story, *Death of a Traveling Salesman*. Bowman, a shoe salesman, traveling in the remote farm country of Mississippi, has a car accident, and he approaches a lone farmhouse. He is tired, unwell, and discouraged. He is met at the door by a suspicious elderly woman who allows him into the house:

"I have a nice line of women's low priced shoes. . ." he said.

But the woman answered, "Sonny'll be here. He's strong. Sonny'll move your car."

"Where is he now?"

"Farms for Mr. Redmond."

Mr. Redmond. Mr. Redmond. That was someone he would never have to encounter, and he was glad. Somehow the name did not appeal to him. . . In a flare of touchiness and anxiety, Bowman wished to avoid even mention of unknown men and their unknown farms.

"Do you live here alone?" He was surprised to hear his old voice chatty, confidential, inflected for selling shoes, asking a question like that—a thing he did not even want to know.

"Yes. We are alone."

Instead of the "saids" and the modifying phrase that would give further meaning to the dialogue, Welty has gone inside Bowman's head. The way he feels, his despair and even his surprise come off better through the interior monologue than they would have if she had substituted a word or two for the "saids."

"Do you live here alone?" he said despairing. . .

"Do you live here alone?" His voice sounded with a
mixture of despair and surprise...

Doesn't Welty do it better? The interior-monologue technique, which we'll get to in Chapter Twelve, is useful, and it can
graphically depict a passage of dialogue.

The rules change a bit, however, when we have more than
two characters in the scene, and all of them speak. Two persons
are fairly easy to keep straight, but three or more mean we have
to use "saids" or their equivalents fairly regularly. In the earlier
Master Key chapter on how dialogue portrays characterizations,
we saw that each speaker must sound different enough so that
the reader can have a perpetually vibrant mental image. Yet
sometimes this just isn't enough, and here is where the "saids"
come in. The main purpose has to be for identification.

In Jimmy Breslin's novel, *Table Money*, we have Owney, in
the army and getting ready to ship out for Viet Nam. He's home
in Queens, and he's at a soda fountain with his friend, Glenn,
and Delores, a woman he has just met (and who is destined to
become his wife). It's a three-way conversation, and the "saids"
appear at the appropriate times:

Owney looked at Delores. "What do you think?"

"I'd hide him in my house."

"Is he your boy friend?"

"No, I'd hide you, too."

"I don't want anybody to hide me," Owney said.

"Then I won't hide you."

"Do you think Glenn is scared?" she asked him.

"I don't talk like that. Glenn is my friend. He can do
anything he wants. Run, hide, fight. Whatever he does is
fine with me. We're cool."

"The only reason I won't hide is I'd get bored staying
under the bed," Glenn said. "I'll go up where there's
tundra."

"All right with me," Owney said.

"I'll send you letters."

"Where from?"

"Where there's ice."

"Who wants to hear about some glacier? I want her to write to me." Owney was looking at Delores.

"I'll write," Delores said . . .

We have no doubt who is saying what at any given moment. No confusion, no uncertainty. The "saids" are dispersed economically throughout the passage, and Breslin allows the dialogue itself to characterize the speaker.

This is the way it should be done.

A writer in complete control of his material.

9

Should He Gesture, Too?

Question: Are there times when fiction and nonfiction writing are barely distinguishable from play writing?

Answer: Absolutely. Stage business, for one thing, must be considered in both cases.

Stage business?

The non-playwright calls it gesturing...

"Thank you," he said, *smiling*.

"Why not?" he said, *with a grin*.

"No way!" he said, *his eyes fierce*.

"Certainly," he said, *handing over the documents*.

D.C. Fontana, former story editor of *Star Trek*, says stage business, or gesturing, includes "a look, or move, a facial expression, a tone of voice, a mood, a pause in speech..." It means that the writer wants to couple some physical action with the dialogue. On the stage this is called "business," as when an actor delivers lines and does something physical at the same time. "Business" is crucial to performance in a play and it is no less crucial on the written page. "Business" is the bridge that ties lines of dialogue together.

For example, if we want to show mild rebuke, we could write:

"You're home late," he said, tapping the pencil on the counter...

The gesture—tapping the pencil—characterizes the dialogue passage and, in fact, underscores it. The tapping pencil is a sign of agitation, and that, in turn, must flow from some element of distress.

There are, basically, four reasons why we use gestures in conjunction with our dialogue:

- to portray character (as in: "I'm leaving now," he said, *kicking in the glass door panels with a vicious swipe*);
- to develop mood (as in: "I won't hurt you" he said, *running a finger across her cheek and neck...*);
- to emphasize a crucial moment in the story (as in: "Leave me alone!" she said, *the tears streaming down her face...*);
- to allow a pause between dialogue passages (as in: "Let's go," he said, *struggling into his leather jacket*. "I mean now!"...).

Gesturing or stage business implies that we want our characters to do more than simply utter unadorned dialogue. We want to inject some form of movement in the scene so things won't—or can't—bog down. On the stage, characters rarely speak their lines without doing *something*—sitting or walking or drinking or making a face—a host of physical mannerisms that complement the spoken word.

The situation should be the same on the written page. Gestures—business—must complement the dialogue.

See how Jayne Ann Phillips does it in her story, *Souvenir*, which is about the relationship between Kate, who is studying for her doctorate, and her mother, who remains in the family home. Kate has just gotten word her mother is in the hospital for tests. She thinks back to the prior summer when the two of them were in the kitchen and her mother was stirring gravy and they were arguing. Her mother speaks:

"Think of what you put yourself through. And how can

you feel right about it? You were born here. I don't care what you say.'' Her voice broke and she looked, perplexed, at the broth in the pan.

"But hypothetically,'' Kate continued, her own voice unaccountably shaking, ''if I'm willing to endure whatever I have to, do you have a right to object? You're my mother. You're supposed to defend my choices.''

"You'll have enough troubles without choosing more for yourself. Using birth control that'll ruin your insides, moving from one place to another. I can't defend your choices. I can't even defend myself against you.'' She wiped her eyes on a napkin.

"Why do you have to make me feel so guilty?'' Kate said, fighting tears of frustration...''

Note the gesturing the author uses here: the mother looks at the broth, perplexed...Kate's voice is shaking...the mother wipes her eyes on a napkin...Kate fights tears of frustration. Each of these points of business serves a basic story purpose. *They emphasize the dialogue itself.*

Mother and daughter are arguing; there is conflict and tension in the scene. Essentially, their argument is about style of life, an ages-old generational conflict. It is certainly a crucial point in the story. The gesturing, then, highlights the disagreement between the two characters; it gives it substance and importance.

Take the final dialogue passage, for instance. "Why do you make me feel guilty?'' Kate said...Do we know the precise frame of mind Kate is in when she says those words? If Jayne Ann Phillips had not added the phrase, *fighting tears of frustration*, we might assume Kate was asking the question at a lower emotional pitch. The words challenge her mother, of course, but there are different levels of challenge, and this one could be less conflict-laden, more like a recurring complaint.

Except when we read the tag line—*fighting tears of frustra-*

tion. Then we know. This is a highly emotional moment. If frustration brings tears to one's eyes, there is deep feeling, and the event is underscored for us.

Suppose we want to create an atmosphere that will amplify and explain our dialogue. Gesturing is an easy way to do it, and it can serve to develop the character of the speakers, as well. If we want to show contentment, for example, we can have a character say:

"Such a meal," he said, *stretching back in the chair...*"

Or if it's uncertainty we want to show:

"My goodness! she said, *reaching out to touch the scarf but drawing her fingers back...*

See how Joseph Conrad does it in his novel, *Under Western Eyes*, the story of Russian exiles in Geneva, Switzerland, during the time of the Tsars. Razumov is a student who has come from Russia to help plot some type of government overthrow in his native land. He and others are at a small meeting in an apartment when the subject of phantoms and apparitions comes up. The atmosphere turns gritty and uncertain:

The tenseness of Madame de S——'s stare had relaxed and now she looked at Razumov in a silence that had become disconcerting.

"I myself have had an experience," he stammered out, as if compelled. "I've seen a phantom once."

The unnaturally red lips moved to frame a question harshly.

"Of a dead person?"

"No. Living."

"A friend?"

"No."

"I hated him."

"Ah! It was not a woman, then?"

"A woman!" repeated Razumov, his eyes looking

straight into the eyes of Madame de S——. "Why should it have been a woman? And why this conclusion? Why should I not have been able to hate a woman?"...

The gesturing here all contributes to making the atmosphere challenging and uncertain...the silence is disconcerting...Razumov stammers, as if compelled...unnaturally red lips frame a question *harshly*...Razumov looking straight into the eyes of Madame de S——...All of these things buttress the words the characters speak, and when Razumov and Madame de S—— parry questions and answers we know it is not a pleasant, friendly conversation. Both are on guard.

Could we have known this if there had been no gesturing? Try reading the dialogue without the stage business; read it out loud and see how it sounds.

Try it, go ahead.

It doesn't seem the same, does it? We need Conrad's gestures in order to get the particular flavor of this scene. Without the gesturing, the uncertainty and the tenseness between the characters don't seem so significant.

And if they're not significant, then what purpose does the scene, itself, have? Not much, really.

Atmosphere, then, and with it elements of characterization, is an important by-product of stage business. Its influence and use should not be ignored.

Still another reason for gesturing is to inject a pause between dialogue passages. Why do we need a pause? We don't want to overwhelm the reader with an avalanche of "he says," "she says," nor do we want to trivialize the dialogue itself. By that we mean offering so much dialogue it just runs together and no passage carries any special significance. Breaking up dialogue by gesturing serves to change the pace and keep the reader's attention.

Take a look at this passage from T. Coraghessan Boyle's novel, *Budding Prospects*, the story of Felix and his friends who have been tending a huge marijuana plot in the uninhabited country north of San Francisco. Their hopes for a major financial killing have been done in by a variety of factors, and Felix now wishes for satisfaction from Vogelsang who put up the money for the land and the cultivating equipment in the first place. Felix suspects Vogelsang has twisted things so he, Vogelsang, will come out ahead.

Suddenly he was on his feet, catty, clonic, the old Vogelsang. He paced to the end of the table and swung around. "I bought that property in February, like I told you. But not this February. February two years ago. You know what I paid?"

I knew nothing. I was a loser.

"Ninety-two."

Chink doom, went the goatherd, *doom-doom*.

"You know what I'm getting—what I got? Already?" The cords stood out in his neck like stitches in a sweater. "I signed over the title yesterday—the deal's been cooking for months. Months." He was twitching, jerking, dancing in place like an Indian whooping over the corpse of an enemy. "One-seventy. And do you know why? Because you improved the place for me."

I sat down. Hard...

The pieces of stage business between the dialogue passages are important because they not only emphasize Vogelsang's self-satisfaction and Felix's despair, but because they make the words even more significant. Vogelsang's coup on the price of the land is all the more galling and triumphant when we see him showing high excitement—he's won, he's won big. By stringing out the revelation, the author has made the triumph even more substantial, and the dialogue passages become the highlights that reveal the triumph. It is simply a more dramatic way of showing the circumstances than it might have been if no gestures were used.

Try the test. Read the dialogue without gestures.

It's not the same, is it?

Several generalities can be drawn about the use of gestures with dialogue. Earlier in the chapter we saw why gestures are used, their application and their value. Now we need to know *how* they should be used.

- Gestures and dialogue should match. (Note the title of this book: *"Shut Up!" He Explained*. This is *not* a match, and Ring Lardner knew it.)
- Too many gestures should be avoided. (The best rule is to limit gesturing to one piece of business per dialogue passage.)
- Gestures should be believable. (The person doing the gesturing must be the kind of person who would do such things. For example, a grief-stricken character would probably *not* break into a broad smile.)
- The gesture should have a purpose. (The writer must ask himself/herself why *this* gesture, why not something else or nothing at all?)

10

Suppose I Want Dialect?

If we've done much writing, aren't we tempted sometimes to slide off standard English usage and try our hands with strange and uncertain diction? I mean, it can be quite different, it can push us into an arena where we're going to have our characters saying things arrestingly, in ways that are unusual.

Dialect can do this, dialogue in dialect.

We have an older man on board ship, and a storm is coming. If we have him speak without dialect, he might say:

> "The sea grows rougher," he said, noting the deepening caverns between the waves...

Now let's make him an old Irish sea dog:

> "Aye, it's makin' up a well-trough of greeney brine, suds're flyin', and' so's me soul..."

Can't we visualize the grizzled old fellow, eyes squinted, pipe clamped between his teeth, almost daring the wind and sea to do him in? His dialect gives him dimension, and this, in turn, gives *us*, the readers, the chance to identify with and emphathize with him.

Dialect usage is important because it can help portray character and storyline. The key is to understand why this happens. Arturo Vivante gives us one good reason:

What a character says should be distinct, should differ from what someone else says, enough to identify him or her immediately and to make it unnecessary for the writer to tell who is speaking.

We have a character speak with a dialect . . . doesn't that make him different, distinct? He speaks, and we know it's *he*! (or *she*!)

Using dialect, however, must be carefully done. It cannot be allowed to flower untended. It will lose its effect quickly and become an impediment to the reader's enjoyment. There are, to be sure, some general guidelines to follow when using dialect with our dialogue, and the best approach is to put them in the form of questions. Suppose we ask ourselves:

- does using dialect have a legitimate purpose in the story?
- am I familiar with the dialect I'm using—am I able to think in this idiom?
- am I limiting my use of dialect to a few key suggestive phrases only?
- am I using dialect to
    a. develop my characters?
    b. change my story pace?

If we can answer honestly in the affirmative, then we are using dialect wisely and well in our dialogue.

See how Wright Morris does it with a passage from *Love Among the Cannibals*, his story of a couple of songwriters and their uncertain adventures in Hollywood and elsewhere. Horter and MacGregor, the song writers, are sunning themselves on a California beach one day when a young woman flops down next to them, opens up a record player, and starts playing one of their songs. They strike up a conversation, though she thinks MacGregor's name is McGraw. The story is seen through Horter's eyes:

"Baby—you sing?"

"Mistuh McGraw!" she said, shocked with recognition.

"Why, Mistuh McGraw."

"Miss—" I began.

"What in the wohld should evah make you think so, Mistah McGraw? Ah do sing. Ah suppose ah should say ah wanna sing."

"Miss Garland—," I said. That clicked. I mean that cut her to the quick.

"Harcum," she said. "Miss Billie Harcum. Ah'm a stootun of Marlene Mazda Joyce, although yuh-all probly know huh, an refuh to huh as somethin' else."

"Muzzy Joyce has some nice contacts, Miss Harcum," I said. "We sometimes find a cage for her little songbirds. You dance?"

"Why Mistuh—"

"Horter. Of MacGregor and Horier."

"Ah'm the awfullust fool, Mistuh Hortuh. Ah know yoh name as well as mah own"'. . .

What's Wright Morris's purpose with this overdrawn dialect? Billie Harcum speaks with a deep southern accent for a particular reason, and Morris portrays it to perfection. Turn the question around—suppose Billie Harcum speaks with *no* southern accent? How does she come across?

Like any young singer on the make, probably. There would be little about her that was special enough for us to want to find out more. Her beach ploy—flopping down next to the song writers and then playing one of their songs—is run-of-the-mill stuff. *Unless* she's sugary sweet, seemingly naive and sooooo embarrassed about it all.

Her character, in other words, is depicted not by her words but by her actions. Watch what I do, don't listen to what I say.

What, then, is Wright Morris's purpose?

Satire, of course. How can a girl who sounds so sweet be as ambitious as this? It takes guts to do what she does, and she holds her ground in spite of the sardonic snapping from Horter. Making Billie Harcum a sugary southerner who exhibits herself in the crassest way tells us that Wright Morris has little use for protestations of innocence. We are all ambitious, he seems to be saying, in spite of ourselves.

Would this passage come off as well, then, if Billie Harcum had not been a sweet-mouthed southerner?

Hardly.

Character development is one of the key reasons for using dialect with dialogue. Something that might have no impact if said in a straightforward manner changes with dialect. It's as if the words become animated and carry a different voice. See how Mark Twain does it with this conversation in *The Adventures of Huckleberry Finn* between Huck and Jim, the liberated black slave. Huck has just told Jim that French people don't talk the same way Americans do, and Jim is perplexed. Huck asks Jim whether a cat or a cow talks like humans do, and Jim admits they don't. Cats and cows don't even talk like one another...

> "It's natural and right for 'em to talk different from each other, ain't it?"
>
> "Course."
>
> "And ain't it natural and right for a cat and a cow to talk different from *us*?"
>
> "Why, mos' sholy is."
>
> "Well, then, why ain't it natural and right for a *Frenchman* to talk different from us. You answer me that."
>
> "Is a cat a man, Huck?"
>
> "No."
>
> "Well, den, dey ain't no sense in a cat talkin' like a man. Is a cow a man—er is a cow a cat?"
>
> "No, she ain't either of them."
>
> "Well, den, she ain't got no business to talk like either er the yuther of 'em. Is a Frenchman a man?"
>
> "Yes."
>
> "Well, den, Dad blame it, why doan he *talk* like a man? You answer me *dat*!"

Jim is obviously uneducated, but his words carry a not-so-subtle message: all men are the same, all men should speak the same language. The principle can be applied as broadly as we wish, but Jim is showing us that his idea of equality is simple and straightforward. Jim's sense of right and wrong belies the dialect and uneducated form of expression he uses. Jim is uttering truth.

And Twain's use of dialect enhances that. The message wouldn't be nearly so effective without the dialect. We perk up our attention at the things Jim says, *precisely because he is the one saying them*. Would they be as effective if said by an educated man with familiar diction?   The analogies would probably be laughable and strain believability, and the effectiveness of the words would lose something.

Jim says it briefly, pointedly, and with drama. His character is delineated by what he says, not by how he says it.

Yet how he says it highlights what he means. The dialect unlocks a facet of his character.

Some of the same rules that apply to dialogue generally also work with dialect. We use dialogue as a change of pace. And we use dialect in the same way. A change of pace in the narrative flow, a change of pace in the dialogue flow:

"I'm looking for little Ben."

"*Inglis*? No?"

"An American boy, ten years old."

"You. *Inglis*. Skeen—light, eye—shine. You."

"American is what I am, chum."

"*Inglis* bad. Boy bad."

"Ben's just a kid, for God's sake . . ."

Note how the dialect interrupts the pace of the dialogue. The speakers don't seem on the same level of understanding, each one talking about something different, and this ragged rhythm produces a sharp contrast which holds our attention. Dialect like this should not be allowed to run on too long because it becomes difficult to follow after a while. Yet, a few passages of barely intelligible dialogue serve the useful purpose of depicting character and holding the spotlight on one of the speakers. As in the case given, the dialect-speaker is showing animosity and telling us something. But if this went on for a page or more, we, the readers, would grow weary of it. The use of dialect, however, does make us take notice of a character in ways we might not otherwise do, and its strange-to-the-ear form keeps us interested—at least for a little while.

In an earlier chapter, we touched on how dialogue can change the pace in a flow of narrative. If we add dialect to the dialogue, the change of pace becomes even sharper. Why would we need such a sharp change of pace? For purposes of characterization, of course, and also to delineate strong contrasts between the speaker and the narration itself. The more erudite the narration, the sharper the contrast with one who speaks in dialect. It becomes a case of double emphasis.

This is what happens in William Faulkner's story, *Pantaloon in Black*, where Rider has just buried his wife and his aunt urges him to come home with her rather than return to an empty house:

> "Whar you gwine?" she said.
>
> "Ah'm goan home," he said.
>
> "You don't wants ter go back by yoself," she said. "You need to eat. You come home and eat."
>
> "Ah'm goan home," he repeated, walking out from under her hands, his forearm like iron, as if the weight on it were no more than that of a fly, the other members of the mill gang whose head he was giving way quietly to let him pass. But before he reached the fence one of them overtook him; he did not need to be told it was his aunt's messenger.
>
> "Wait Rider," the other said. "We gots a jug in de bushes.". . .

Note the contrast between the simple dialect and the straight narration. The narration changes the pace of the dialogue, the dialogue does the same to the narration, yet both are ultimately influenced by the dialect which adds flavor to the suffering

Rider feels. He may not say much, but we know—we feel—his suffering at this moment. The simplicity of what the characters say lends eloquence to what they are feeling. It isn't necessary to write a drawn-out scene on grief and misery and pain. The words, *"Ah'm goan home"* say it all.

And that is why dialect can be so useful. It can accomplish much in a short space, and it can lend a special reality to what our characters say.

Providing we remember two things:

- don't overdo the use of dialect;
- don't use dialect we aren't completely familiar with.

Got that, y'all?

11

What About Transitions and Flashbacks?

What do all of these have in common?

"You better be there tomorrow where I can see you..."

"Guess how far we've come these past two weeks..."

Two days later he said...

They imply *change*. There has been or will be disruption in the storyline. A period of time has passed or will pass between events.

Phrases like this are known as transitions, and they are a common technique for highlighting the passage of time. Most stories pass through events in such a way that periods of time must be accounted for as unobtrusively as possible. These time periods may have only peripheral influence on the storyline, yet if they are ignored, the reader could be confused.

So, we employ a transitional device to alert the reader that a period of time will be passing. The most usual vehicle for this is the standard time-passing phrases: *The next day...One month later...It was six months before...* And dialogue is a handy adjunct to all of this. *One month later he said...* We can even begin the transitional passage with dialogue:

"You didn't act this way two weeks ago when..."

The point is that we must highlight the change, and dialogue, by virtue of its dramatic effect, can do this easily. It doesn't matter whether the change takes place in hours, days, weeks, months, or years, dialogue will bring the flavor of immediacy to the act of transition. In doing this it will lend credibility to the fact that there has been a change and that things have occurred during that change which probably have little effect on our storyline. What the characters are saying *now* is the important thing. The transition has given us a leap through time.

Generally, however, dialogue has a difficult time if it is in both ends of the transition. It's hard to mesh properly two different stages of dialogue without some device for intervention. The reason should be apparent: because dialogue carries such a strong sense of immediacy, two passages, one right after the other, must have something inserted so their time-relevance can be distinguished.

There are two ways, at least, to do this:
  - use a narrative insertion, such as *One month later . . .* ;
  - skip several lines, leaving space in the manuscript, separating the two sections so that different periods of time are apparent.

There is, also, a third technique which can—though it doesn't have to—combine the two above. Dialogue is especially helpful here: simply allow our dialogue passage to provide a clue or an insight about the coming transition. If we do this, we don't have to use a narrative insertion defining the passage of time, nor do we have to separate our text or mark out a different scene. This is what W. Somerset Maugham does with his story, *The Colonel's Lady*. One of his lead characters, a well-known British author, is complaining about a publisher's promotion efforts for his latest book. A cocktail party has been arranged, and the author is attempting to convince a friend to attend:

"I expect it'll be very dull, but they're making rather a point of it. And the day after, the American publisher who's taken my book is giving a cocktail party at Claridge's. I'd like you to come to that, if you wouldn't mind."

"Sounds like a crashing bore, but if you really want me to come I'll come."

"It would be sweet of you."

George Peregrine was dazed by the cocktail party...

Note how the dialogue anticipates the transition. The conversation speaks of the cocktail party that's to come in the future, and so the reader is alerted that a time period is about to pass. Maugham doesn't bother skipping lines when he writes: *George Peregrine was dazed*...nor does he need to insert: *Two days later George Peregrine was dazed*...The clues in the dialogue made all that unnecessary. The time change has occurred simply, easily, with the reader in step.

Flashbacks, like transitions, also call for change, and similar techniques can be used. It's important to understand, though, that while all flashbacks are transitions, the reverse is not true; all transitions are not flashbacks, or put another way, flashbacks are but one form of transition.

All writers use flashbacks, and they are a most useful device. They can give body to a story, provide motivation, flesh out characterization, even offer a moral imperative which can become a central theme. But flashbacks need to be handled properly, and, when dialogue is involved, that means understanding the sense of immediacy that will be injected into the story.

We've all gone to the most usual flashback techniques...*I heard the music and it reminded me*...*That nasal telephone voice took me back to*..."*Tell me about the time that*..." I call these "memory lane" devices, and they are perfectly appropriate for a story.

In using them—or any other method—there are some general principles we should keep in mind.

- Flashbacks require careful use of tenses; it may be necessary to start with a past tense, but things should be brought to the present tense as quickly as possible to preserve the sense of immediacy.

- Flashbacks must be relevant to the action; they must play an integral part in the story.
- Flashbacks should occasion no break in the story flow; if the reader has to go back and forth to understand where he/she is in the story, the flashback isn't of much use.
- Flashbacks need not be provided in just one segment; portions can be applied throughout the story, *if* it contributes to the telling of the story.

Let's look at one of the twentieth century's finest pieces of literature, Robert Penn Warren's *All the King's Men*. The story takes place in Louisiana. Jack Burden, the narrator, is assistant to Willie Stark, the Governor. Burden has been told by Stark to go to Mason City and find something derogatory about Judge Irwin who has become a political obstacle. As the next chapter opens, Burden remembers the last time he had been sent to Mason City, seventeen years before...

> The managing editor of the *Chronicle* called me in and said, "Jake get in your car and go up to Mason City and see who the hell that fellow Stark is who thinks he is Jesus Christ scourging the money-changers out of the shinplaster courthouse up there."
>
> "He married a school teacher," I said.
>
> "Well, it must have gone to his head," Jim Madison, who was managing editor of the *Chronicle*, said. "Does he think he is the first one ever popped a schoolteacher?"
>
> "The bond issue was for building a schoolhouse," I said, "and it looks like Lucy figures they might keep some of it for that purpose."
>
> "Who the hell is Lucy?"
>
> "Lucy is the schoolteacher," I said.

The key here is the immediacy of the dialogue. This conversation is taking place *now*, even though Warren made it plain it actually occurred seventeen years before. The immediacy, however, comes from the verb tenses Warren uses...*I said...Jim Madison said*...rather than *I had said*, etc. In this way Warren makes us understand that Burden and Madison are speaking in a contemporary frame. See how the technique works: going to Mason City makes Burden remember (the "memory lane" device); the first passage of dialogue uses "said" and from that point we have the sense of the present tense; and everything spoken is taking place as we read. Our awareness is not of a past event but of a current conversation. Then, when Warren wants to pull Burden back to the real present, he simply has him stop remembering. An important thing to catch here is the insight this flashback scene also provides into the character of Willie Stark. We find out his wife was a schoolteacher, we find out who gave him the information about construction defects in the school building, and we find out how he used this information. By preserving the sense of immediacy in the dialogue, Warren has made the revelation about Stark's character more dramatic—and more interesting.

Suppose we write:

> Thirty years ago I *had had* the same experience. My father *had* been there to see it. "Look!" he *had* said. "A cloud in the shape of the devil!"
>
> "Does it mean bad luck?" I *had* asked.
>
> "Your mother would call it a sign of evil," he *had* scoffed...

All of this is in the past tense, and the element of immediacy is certainly reduced. It may still read dramatically, but it probably would read more dramatically if we got into the present as quickly as possible. The opening line of the flashback could remain: *Thirty years ago I had had*...but after that we could write...*I said...I asked...he scoffed*...and have immediacy back again.

This is the way John Steinbeck does it in a scene from his book *The Winter of Our Discontent*. Ethan Allen Hawley lives in New England and is beset by pressures from his wife and family to live a better life, one that would require him to compromise some of his moral values. He recalls the death of his brother-in-law the year before, a death he witnessed, and the sudden horrifying apparition that appeared before him, and his urge to bite out the apparition's throat:

> When it was over, in panic quiet, I confessed what I had felt to old Doc Peele, who signed the death certificate.
>
> "I don't think it's unusual," he said. "I've seen it on people's faces, but few admit it."
>
> "But what causes it? I liked him."
>
> "Might be an old memory," he said. "Maybe a return to the time of the pack when a sick or hurt member was in danger. Some animals and most fish tear down and eat a weakened brother."
>
> "But I'm not an animal—or a fish."
>
> "No, you're not. And perhaps that's why you find it foreign. But it's there. It's all there."
>
> He's a good man, Doc Peele, a tired old man. He's birthed and buried us for years...

Note that Steinbeck uses the past tense to get us into the flashback...what I *had* felt...but after this it's all the present tense. As Doc Peele and Ethan discuss the apparition and its normal occurrence, they might as well be speaking in front of us. There is no indication—except for the original flashback entry—that the conversation took place one year before. The drama in the passage bursts upon us because it is immediate. It's as if we're spectators at a live production, and we're hearing every word.

Then when Steinbeck wants to take us out of the flashback, he moves away from the dialogue into a narrative of Doc Peele and gradually, easily, we are brought back to the present... *He's birthed and buried us for years* ...The next sentence could begin with dialogue or narrative, but we can be back in the present without anything further. Steinbeck has given us a bridge, and with a word like *now*, or a phrase to indicate contemporaneity such as *All of that was a year ago*, we're out of the flashback.

As with any story device, we have to make sure the flashback fits in well with the story we are writing. The flashback must serve a purpose; it must highlight character, advance the plot or develop the story theme in some way. It must, in other words, *fit in*.

Dialogue without good purpose is, as we've seen in an earlier chapter, static writing. Nothing moves, nothing lives.

So, in our flashback, the dialogue must do something to the story.

See how Mary Lee Settle does it with *The Killing Ground*. Hannah, now a famous author, has returned to her West Virginia home, and an old friend, Kitty Puss, has just called her with a drunken outpouring of invective at how Hannah embarrassed everyone during the 1960s with her liberal, civil rights views. Notice, in the following passage, how Settle uses the "memory lane" flashback device:

> Kitty Puss had called up an old trial and I was back within it. A headline in the morning paper. "Local writer leads march..." My father was striking the paper against his hand while he stood at the door of my apartment at seven o'clock in the morning. He strode into the room without looking at me. How did he begin? I only heard again "...Some consideration for our place in the community...under no circumstances are you ever to humiliate us again..." as if I were sixteen instead of thirty-eight years old...

In this passage, we have only snatches of the dialogue, but it is enough to give us the flavor of the scene. The flashback erupts because of a conflict ("the old trial") and continues into conflict between Hannah and her father.

But the real key is what it tells us about the relationship between Hannah and her parents and about Hannah's political views. This is character development in the primary sense because we learn things we never knew before, not only about Hannah and her parents but about Kitty Puss. The characters come to life.

The storyline develops.

The flashback is. . .relevant.

12

Suppose I Want to Talk to Myself?

"You are the one who writes, and the one who is written."
Edmond Jabes offered that a number of years ago in his *The
Book of Questions*. He is referring to a writing technique where
we talk to ourselves about ourselves in the privacy of our own
psychic pastures.

It is dialogue with only one talker and one listener, a stage
with only one performer.

People call it stream of consciousness or interior monologue
(essentially they are the same thing), and it is the process of
entering the mind of a character and witnessing the psychic life
cycle of a portion of that character's existence.

Bruce Kawin puts it well. Stream of consciousness, he says:

> . . . has come to refer to a method of presenting, as if
> directly and without mediation, the flowing or jagged se-
> quence of the thoughts, perceptions, preconscious associa-
> tion, memories, half realized impressions, and so on, of
> one or more characters—the attempt, in fiction, to imitate
> the complete mental life as it manifests itself in the ongo-
> ing present.

In simplest terms, it means we have characters thinking and
talking to themselves about what they are thinking.

Stream of consciousness has been used for many years by some of the finest writers: Virginia Wolff, Marcel Proust, Gertrude Stein, Samuel Beckett, Manuel Puig, among others. It is a way of delving into characterization far beyond the limits of objective portrayal. We can get to know the characters so much better.

Think of it...Usual dialogue is limited by what people actually say to one another. Not so with stream of consciousness. We can have the characters thinking much more broadly, much more deeply than would be shown by what we could have them say out loud.

"I hate you!" she said.

We might know why she hates from what she has said earlier, or we might figure it out from things that have happened to her in the course of the story. But if we use stream of consciousness, we would know, not only why she hates, but what effect it might have on her moral balance, whether she's ever hated before, how it might affect her behavior towards others, what philosophical give-and-take she has encountered or will encounter, what role hating can play in her life as well as in the lives of others, and so forth.

We read it from her perspective, and when we're finished, there isn't much about her we don't know.

James Joyce was one of the foremost practitioners of the stream-of-consciousness technique, and in his novel, *Ulysses*, he employs it over and over. Joyce, however, isn't content with simple declarative phrasing: he offers a sometimes-poetic, sometimes-obtuse, sometimes-unfinished thought style which could reflect the true psychic process in motion.

See how he handles his lead character, Stephan Dedalus, and his impressions of the moment of awareness. Does Dedalus see things first or does he feel them?

> Ineluctable modality of the visible: at least that if no more, thought through my eyes. Signature of all things I am here to read, seapawn and seawrack, the nearing tide,

that rusty boat. Snotgreen, bluesilver, rust: coloured signs, Limits of the diaphone. But he adds: in bodies, then he was aware of them bodies before of them coloured. How? By knocking his sconce against them, sure. Go easy. . .

These are seemingly disjointed thoughts, but there is an actual pattern to them. Joyce is showing that the eye can take in only so much, that the other senses have to take over in order to make a complete picture. This is what is going through Dedalus's head; the thoughts are flying around like electrons inside the atom. Yet the process produces the desired result; don't we know Stephan Dedalus better than if Joyce had written:

"Tell me what you see."

"What I feel, you mean. Seeing comes later."

Objective dialogue may give us the message, but stream of consciousness gives the message substance and flavor. When we talk to ourselves, we are simply less inhibited. Note how Joyce is not bound by pronoun conventions. He uses "I" and "my" interchangeably with "he." It's all the same person. As the mind flicks from concept to concept, phrase to phrase, isn't the change of pronoun perfectly logical?

What Joyce's style says is this: the mind itself is not subject to an editor's blue pencil. It can't be and remain in psychic freedom. If it is truly stream of consciousness, it must be allowed to flow unimpeded.

Most writers use this technique only sparingly, and even then, they avoid the total free flow that Joyce gives us. Sentences are more conventional, vocabulary more every-day, but the purpose is still the same: to probe the limits of the mind through the free association of thoughts.

When we talk to ourselves, we seek answers, or at least partial answers. We want to know something, we want to understand something. Stream of consciousness is a way of letting us learn more.

Answers, we want answers.

So, we ask questions.

It's a most appropriate stream-of-consciousness technique. Questions and answers.

See how Gail Godwin does it with her novel, *A Mother and Two Daughters*. Nell is in her garden, remembering times long past. A widow, she is entering a comfortable old age, content in her relationship with her daughters and the close family ties.

> ...If only we were not mortal, she thought; if only we were not personal, there would be so much less pain. But how do I know that? This flower is not mortal, it is not personal. But if I wrenched off its taut, prim petals, if I snatched the bulb from its hole and left it lying to bake in the sun, to die, it would feel its own kind of pain and betrayal. Would I prefer to be this crocus and take my chances on suffering its kind of pain? Even if I could live longer than the human being who planted me, even if I could be spared the human pains of memory, or anxiety about the future?...

Nell explores her own feelings about mortality, and she does it by asking herself—how and what if? *How do I know that?... what if I snatched the bulb...what if I could be the crocus?...*

She anwers these questions with one simple word:

No.

The question approach is hardly new, yet it remains a most useful way of handling stream of consciousness. We talk to ourselves, we ask and we answer, and in this way we explore the psychic realm. Many people refer to the question technique as "Socratic dialogue," meaning that the true answers come only after we question, question, question. The first answer, even the tenth answer, might not be sufficient, but with each question and answer, we come closer and closer to what we seek.

The point is that stream of consciousness (or interior monologue) probes the reaches of the psyche in an effort to show us the truest nature of the character. Edouard Desjardin wrote that interior monologue is "the speech of a character in a scene, having for its object to introduce us directly into the interior life of that character, without author intervention through explanation or commentaries."

The interior life of the character.

Doesn't the question technique operate well here? How better to expose a character's interior life than to have him or her ask themselves personal questions and then answer them?

Desjardin goes on, "...it is an expression of the most intimate thought that lies nearest the unconscious..."

The most intimate thought!

But did I...?

Suppose I...?

How can I...?

Why should I...?

Sometimes, stream of consciousness comes off better when we stay away from the first person—I or we—and use the second person—you. Then, it's—you think...you don't...you will ...you can't...and the feeling comes across that it's just the teeniest less intimate because things are more declarative and less conversational.

Isn't this what it seems like in Ernest Hemingway's *For Whom The Bell Tolls*? Robert Jordan, an American fighting with the Republican forces in the Spanish Civil War, is part of a guerilla band planning to blow up a key bridge. He thinks about his responsibilities to the other members of the group:

> So you say that it is not that which will happen to yourself but that which may happen to the woman and the girl and to the others that you think of. All right. What would have happened to them if you had not come? What happened to them and what passed with them before you were ever here? You must not think in that way. You have no responsibility for them except action. The orders do not come from you. They come from Golz. And who is Golz? A good general. The best you've served under. But should a man carry out impossible orders knowing what they lead to?...

Obviously, here too, Hemingway uses the question technique, but note he stays with "you." It's as if he wants Jordan to square his shoulders and stop thinking and acting in some less acceptable way. Hemingway has Jordan rap himself across the psychic knuckles—*you must not think...you have no responsibility...*

Try it in the first person. *I must not think...I have no responsibility...* it doesn't feel the same, it doesn't command the same attention.

Using the second person gives the explanation strength, as if another individual is inside the character's head, wagging a finger and giving encouragement. It's hard to visualize the same thing when we use the first person.

Stream of consciousness presents a rich canvas upon which to portray a story. As we talk to ourselves, we can develop a number of themes, all of which lend substance and variety. We should not make the mistake of assuming that just because stream-of-consciousness writing *seems* to mirror narration, it can't be flexible enough to do what objective dialogue does best—give a sense of immediacy and drama to the script.

Objective dialogue can show characters with all their warts; it can present them as caricatures or as heroes; it can turn them into objects of derision and ridicule as well as into instruments of mockery and irony.

But so can stream of consciousness.

See how Jerzy Kozinski does it in his novel, *Pinball*. It is the story of Goddard, a highly acclaimed rock musician whom no one has ever seen. Domostroy is a famous composer, and he has fallen for Andrea, who is using him to find Goddard. Domostroy has just received an offer in the mail to join a vasectomy club:

Domostroy stopped to think. If he should ever undergo a vasectomy—although he could imagine nothing less likely—what right would he have to proselytize? Furthermore, if in search of external identity—again, a concept quite foreign to him—he should decide to define himself as an American Vasectomite, where would he feel confident wearing the National Vasectomy Club lapel pin or the tie tack? To cocktails? To dinner with a date? To church? And what about the membership card? Why and where would he need it? To whom could he show it? He imagined being stopped by the highway patrol for speeding and saw himself producing, in addition to his driver's license, his National Vasectomy card . . .

This, of course, is satire, and it's done as Domostroy talks with himself. The question technique is apparent and useful, and note how the questions take us further and further from the reality of a simple vasectomy. Kozinski is skewering mail-order club memberships, the American penchant for club joining, the inclination to proselytize, the urge for self-confession and self-expression . . . Kozinski seems to be saying: *is it really necessary to tell the world everything! Must I share it all*?

The point is that by portraying the ridiculous lengths to which such a thing can go, he shows us its essential flaws. This is fine satire.

It also shows us ingredients of Domostroy's character. We see the level of his modesty, as well as the sardonic cut of his wit. We come to know him better.

And it's because we can see him talk to himself!

13

What If It's a Short Story? A Novel?

Suppose we tell the tale of a man and woman and their marriage? It is breaking up, though only one of them is conscious of it. We want to portray why and how and when, and we want to show the essential incompatibility.

Could we do this with a short story?

Could we do this with a novel?

The answer, of course, is yes to both questions; but the story, obviously, would be structured differently. Some years ago, L.A.G. Strong gave us the short story approach:

> The modern short story writer is content if, allowing the reader to glance at his characters as through a window, he shows them making a gesture which is typical: that is to say, a gesture which enables the reader's imagination to fill in all that is left unsaid. Instead of giving us a finished action to admire, or pricking the bubble of some problem, he may give us only the key piece of a mosaic, around which, if sufficiently perceptive, we can see in shadowy outline the completed pattern.

In our dissolving-marriage situation, we might have the characters say:

"Would you like eggs Benedict for lunch?" she asked.

"Did you see the paper this morning?"

"I haven't touched it."

"I mean, did you *read* it?"

"I wish the newsprint wouldn't come off on my fingers. Ugh!"

"Never mind."

"Let's have sliced tomatoes, too...."

This is short-story-dialogue writing. Quick, pointed, letting us observe a lack of communication. If two or three more passages like this were all that appeared in the story, we would be able to grasp a picture of the incompatibility in the marriage. The short-story writer doesn't attempt to lay it all out, but aims to present a flavor which we can then extend in our imaginations.

Now, if the same sentiments were to appear in a novel, they might take this form:

"Would you like eggs Benedict for lunch?" she asked.

"Long memory, you have."

"We haven't had them for months."

"How about yesterday?"

"Not so, darling. You never even made it home for dinner, remember?"

"Cholesterol. I'm talking about that. You said our diets should change."

"And our drinking habits, too, I said..."

This is *not* short-story writing. No doubt we might sense the seeds of animosity between the couple, but this passage needs to be more fully fleshed out before we can say there is incompatibility. All we have above is some polite conflict with maybe, maybe, a deeper strain. It is not so pointed, and it shows there is a history to the individual passages of dialogue (for example, has their drinking been a problem through the marriage?). In effect, for this passage to mean something, we would need to know a great deal more, while for the short-story passage, the dialogue we have should tell us a good share of what we need to know.

If we need to put it into images, here's how Arturo Vivante would do it:

> ...Not only does a short story have a different length, it also has a different pace from a novel. A novel is the sustained flight of geese from Labrador to Florida, a short story, the flight of a sparrow across a fence from field to field.

There are some generalities we can make about writing dialogue for short stories and for novels. Basically, we set up the rules for short stories because the limitations are so much more severe. Anything that doesn't fit within these rules then becomes appropriate for the novel.

We should remember:

- to use dialogue when portraying character in short stories; narrative portrayal is not effective;
- to make short-story dialogue *of the moment*; don't carry the action back for days or forward for days;
- to have short-story dialogue teach only bits and pieces of characters; don't attempt to depict the entire person;
- to have short-story dialogue seek only simple truths; don't have the characters look for cosmic answers.

See how we come to know the characters in Penelope Gilliatt's short story, *On Each Other's Time*, and what we find out in such a short space. Two brothers are speaking on the telephone as the story opens:

> "Are you as low as I am?" said Alfred Rowlett, aged thirty-four, yelling cheerfully on the telephone from Bolivia at eight thirty-five in the morning.
>
> "I don't know how that is," shouted his brother Frederick, aged thirty-two, from Madras, where it was five past six in the evening.
>
> "About the riots," said Alfred.
>
> "Where you are or where I am?" said Frederick.

"In Liverpool," said Alfred.

"Probably lower, though I'm more resilient," said Frederick who had polio. "I can hear your breakfast coming in."

"That isn't breakfast, that's my bed. They don't do breakfast here. They bring the bed instead. I suppose so that they don't have to make it because it's gone again in the evening. I have to sleep on the floor. I have to wait for it in the morning and tip them, because otherwise they make a mess of my notes."

We come to know these characters quickly, and this, of course, is the essence of the short story. If we had been reading a novel, the dialogue would have been more slowly paced, perhaps with passages of narrative, but certainly with less frenetic character depiction. In fact, such a story might never have begun with a telephone call at all. There would have been no need to rush right into the situation, events could have proceeded more slowly and with lengthier examination. Instead of a sparrow flying from post to post, we could have had a flock of geese on a cross-country migration.

Which is precisely the way dialogue is written in Robert Wilder's *Affair of Honor*. Jan Hartog and her father, Maximilian, live in splendor on Lyford Cay in the Bahamas. They have power and money, and they are ruthless with those who oppose them. Jan meets Sherry Melnick who is doing real estate work for her father, though the two men have never laid eyes on one another. Jan begins an affair with Sherry, and they are flying in from Miami. The plane is luxuriously appointed:

"It impresses a lot of people." Jan studied him. "Somehow I didn't think it would impress you."

"It doesn't. Not the way you mean. It's the power it represents." He changed the subject. It would be difficult to explain what he meant. "Do you really want me to stay at your place?"

"Are you afraid of the old man?"

"No. Curious."

"We may not even see him. It's that sort of household. We sometimes go days at a time without running into each other. Lately, though, he has been softening up a little, getting paternal, worrying about my future. Do you know?" The notion interested her. "The two of you might like each other." She broke off.

"Until he finds I'm a Jew?"

"You don't have to be so damned offensive, so ready to be challenged. Are you always this way, looking for trouble?"

The dialogue here does give us insights into characterization. We learn, for example, that Sherry carries a medium-sized chip on his shoulder and that another man's power and authority are not to be feared, but understood. We find, also, that Jan sees her father as a comfortable protection and as an instrument to measure others with. But the more important thing to note is the matter of *time* in the sequence of dialogue. Time is moving here. The story is not like a block of ice cut from a huge, frozen mountain, to be flavored and lost in a moment. Time is running on ahead of the characters as well as moving off behind them. It controls what the characters say to one another, why and where they say it.

Take a look at what's implied in Wilder's words: Sherry will meet Maximilian *at some point in the future*; Jan will probably ask her father why he's getting paternal *at some point in the future*; Sherry will probably talk about why he carries a chip on his shoulder, *something that happened in the past* . . . the story, in other words, does not begin and end with just a few events in the lives of these people. The story—the novel—covers a good deal of ground, and time, therefore, moves forward and backward to reflect all this.

But see how Penelope Gilliatt did it with her story. Even with the opening dialogue we can sense that time is *of the moment*, that what the brothers say to one another reflects only that which is going on *right now*. The story can't move into the past or project much into the future because then it will lose character as a short story. Dialogue must do the same thing: when we're writing short stories, the words must be an accurate portrayal of things happening *right now*, without thought of covering future or past events, except in passing. Dialogue must speak *now*.

Dialogue must also tell us a lot in a short space, if it's a short story. Gilliat did that well with her story, as does A.E. Coppard with his *A Field of Mustard*. Rose and Dinah are returning from picking firewood in the forest, and Rose mentions how she envies Dinah and her children.

"They're good children. Dinah, yours are. And they make you a valentine, and give you a ribbon on your birthday, I expect?"

"They're naught but a racket from cockcrow till the old man snores—and then it's worse."

"Oh, but the creatures, Dinah!"

"You—you get your quiet, trim house, and only your man to look after, a kind man, and you'll set with him in the evenings and play your dominoes or your draughts, and he'll look at you—the nice man—over the board, and stroke your hand now and then."

The wind hustled the two women close together, and as they stumbled under their burdens Dinah Lock stretched out a hand and touched the other woman's arm. "I like you, Rose, I wish you were a man..."

Note the short takes here. Dinah has little use for her husband, and she finds her children a nuisance. She would prefer to live in a quiet house with someone who was kind and who would look after her. Rose, on the other hand, sees Dinah with her children, something she would love to have but doesn't. What we have in this little passage is well portrayed cross-envy, each wishing to be in the other's shoes. We learn it quickly, sharply, easily. The dialogue is pointed and immediate, which is what it is supposed to be in a short story.

And if this story had been a novel? Each element of dissatisfaction could have had a scene or two to itself, and a conversation such as the one above would have been almost anti-climactic.

Novels do cover a lot of ground, and for that reason the stories can develop more substantial thoughts and ideas. A short story may show us a simple truth about human nature, but novels can highlight the truth, the essentials of who we are and why we do the things we do. Look at it this way: a short story may show that a person's good looks won't necessarily reflect a good heart, while a novel will show why that is and why we tend to want the good heart and the good looks to coincide.

Novels can think in big ways, and their dialogue can reflect that. William Kennedy in his novel, *Ironweed*, set in the 1930s, shows us this. For the past fourteen years Francis Phelan has been a hobo, a bum, having fled his native Albany after killing a man in the midst of a labor dispute in 1919. Now he is back in Albany, but he spends his time in the hobo jungle among those he is most comfortable with. He is speaking to his pal, Rudy, who asks why people call them both bums:

"I can't understand why."

"They feel better when they say it."

"The truth ain't gonna hurt you," Francis said. "If you're a bum, you're a bum."

"It hurt a lotta bums. Ain't many of the old ones left."

"There's new ones comin' along," Francis said.

"A lot of good men died. Good mechanics, machinists, lumberjacks."

"Some of 'em ain't dead," Francis said. "You and me, we ain't dead."

"They say there's no God," Rudy said. "But there must be a God. He protects bums. . ."

Two major thoughts are revealed here: there is a sadistic streak to human nature; people grow in self-importance when they build themselves up at another's expense; good and bad aren't decided by the cut of a man's finances; God can approve of a man even if he is a bum. These are cosmic thoughts, and they belong in a novel where they can be expanded upon, debated, even highly criticized. Such effort would have no place in a short story because the subjects are simply too substantial for the medium. Note here, too, that dialogue, not narration, presents the thoughts. It is dialogue that is speaking with a cosmic voice.

Alberto Moravia, the Italian novelist, gives us a good perspective: "The novel," he says, "has a bone structure holding it together from top to toe, whereas the short story is, so to speak, boneless."

Think Big!...says the novelist.

Think Now!...says the short-story writer.

14

Suppose I Want Dialogue Within Dialogue?

Conversation is but carving!
Give no more to every guest
Than he's able to digest.
Give him always of the prime,
And but little at a time.
Carve to all but just enough,
Let them neither starve nor stuff,
And that you may have your due,
Let your neighbor carve for you...

This little ditty is by Jonathan Swift, and, appropriately enough, it's found in his essay, *Conversations*, written more than two hundred and fifty years ago. If we exchange "dialogue" for the word "conversation" in the first line (I know—in the beginning of the book we decided dialogue was *not* conversation, and it isn't, but bear with me), it gives us some of the elusive secrets to writing good dialogue.

Give no more to every guest/Than he's able to digest: keep the dialogue sparse and lean, don't overwhelm the reader... *Give him always of the prime*: the dialogue must mean something, it must do something...*And but little at a time*:

ration the dialogue so the reader looks for more...*Let them neither starve nor stuff*: manage the pace of the dialogue, keep it even and in rhythm...*Let your neighbor carve for you*: cast a reader's critical eye on the dialogue that's been written; make sure it meets the tests we've just gone through.

No, conversation is not dialogue, but they have enough resemblance so we can learn a few things by interchanging them. Swift's verse isn't telling us how to write dialogue, he's prescribing how to talk in public and carry on a conversation. Swift, after all, was a social critic, and conversation—or its unsatisfactory attempt—is a social convention. But the rules of conversation for Swift fit well with the rules of dialogue: keep it lean, keep it under control, keep it purposeful. If we think in Swift's image of lean carvings off a block of meaty social interaction—it might be simpler to remember.

Following this metaphor is especially important when we're faced with what some call "interior dialogue."

Dialogue within dialogue.

First thing to understand: interior dialogue is *not* the same as interior monologue. Interior monologue is talking to ourselves; interior dialogue is talking with others. Conceivably, interior dialogue could include interior monologue, but not the other way around.

Suppose we have two characters talking, and one is relating a story:

"Strange thing, Bobby, the way the car was runnin', and Harry, there, just smilin' at the road, goin' seventy-five, suckin' in the sun. 'Hey!' I yell, 'you notice the shimmy?' 'Nope.' He shakes his head, pats the dash. 'Car's a road hugger, old reliable.' 'What about that!' I yell. 'Feel that!' Vibrations are rattlin' our teeth. 'The wind,' he shouts, smiles. 'Gusty today'...."

This is interior dialogue, a story within another passage of dialogue, and there are times when it is most effective. But it must be handled delicately so that the main dialogue passage won't lose its meaning and effect. We don't want to pour too much into the interior dialogue and leave the underlying dialogue gasping for breath.

Remember Jonathan Swift! He gives us three keepsakes:
- keep it lean;
- keep it under control;
- keep it purposeful.

Follow these, and the interior dialogue can blossom with poise and drama.

When do we use interior dialogue? It is not appropriate for all circumstances, but sometimes it works well. Perhaps the most common use is in dealing with characters and events that lend themselves to dialect portrayal. "Argot" in the vocabulary of critics and reviewers—slang and colloquialisms. "Lingo" to us. It isn't just an occasional word or phrase; it's an entire manner of speaking.

See how Sarah Orne Jewett, who wrote of her beloved Maine and its people, did it in a sketch of a family reunion in her lengthy portrayal, *The Country of Pointed Firs*. Mrs. Todd is speaking of her husband's cousin who appears at the reunion:

"You wouldn't think such a great creature's I be could feel all over pins and needles. I remember, the day I promised to Nathan, how it came over me, just's I was feelin' happy's I could, that I'd get to have an own cousin o' his for my near relation all the rest o' my life, an' it seemed as if die I should. Poor Nathan saw somethin' had crossed me—he had very nice feelings—and when he asked me what 't was, I told him. 'I never could like her myself,' said he. 'You sha'n't be bothered, dear,' he says; an 't was one o' the things that made me set a good deal by Nathan, he didn't make a habit of always opposin' like some men. 'Yes,' says I, 'but think o' Thanksgivin' times an' funerals; she's our relation, an' we've got to own her!' Young folks don't think o' those things...."

Note two things here: there is added dramatic value from the interior dialogue between Mrs. Todd and Nathan, and the dialect gives it a special authenticity. This isn't some outlander attempting to mirror the way the people talked, it is a native telling a story in a native tongue. The passage reeks of authenticity. Jewett is careful to keep her characters in line, and when they speak through interior dialogue, they maintain the "lingo" of the overall scene—*you sha'n't be bothered...we've got to own her...*We should pay as much attention to the dialect in the interior dialogue as we do to the dialect in the underlying dialogue; they must mesh smoothly.

Willa Cather shows us why this type of writing—this "argot" —can mean so much:

> The 'sayings' of a community, its proverbs, are its characteristic comment upon life; they imply its history, suggest its attitude toward the world, and its way of accepting life. Such an idiom makes the finest language any writer can have...

Poor Nathan saw somethin' had crossed me...

He didn't make a habit of always opposin'...

We've got to own her...

When we have characters speak in this fashion, it isn't only the authenticity that we appreciate, it's the fact that no writer could invent it properly. It is beyond our creative powers to develop such a complex lingo and keep it going. Only where the writer's ear can pick up the dialect and become totally familiar with it long before he or she writes it, does the language resound with truth and realism.

Interior dialogue is a true test of our familiarity with the language we seek to employ. It's one thing to have a character use unmodified dialogue, but it's something else to have that same character relate another conversation within the context of that underlying dialogue. The internal dialogue has to be consistent with the speech patterns the character has already shown, and it must do something for the story—either develop characterization further or push the plot along.

This is the way George Higgins approaches his work. Most of

his fiction is in dialogue, and as the characters speak, the story is developed. Frequently, he uses interior dialogue because his characters must describe other events that form part of the story. In *Kennedy for the Defense*, his protagonist, Jerry Kennedy, is listening to a client, Teddy Franklin, describe being stopped by a Massachusetts state trooper who proceeds to *eat* his license and then arrest him for driving without a license. The same week, the trooper stops Franklin's wife and eats her registration and then arrests her, as well. Teddy refers to his brother-in-law, Jake, who is a civilian but is well connected with the police:

"Then I tell Jake about my license. 'He doin' this to her, account of you?'' Jake says. I tell him, 'Sure!' Jake says, 'I dunno this guy. I gotta find out who this guy is. There's gotta be somethin' wrong with him, he's doin' things like this, and if there's somethin' wrong with him, there's gotta be somebody around I knew, knows about it.'

Which,'' Teddy said, "is how I find out about the knife''. . .

The speech patterns are consistent here, and as Jake talks, we can visualize him. Teddy is a small-time hustler, so the story he tells about his brother-in-law must reflect his talk-from-the-side -of-the-mouth mannerism, his colloquialisms and his ability to tell a good story. Does Higgins succeed in this?

Try to write the passage without the colloquial words, phrases, and style. . .*I don't know this man*. . .*I must find out who he is*. . .*There must be something wrong with him*. . .

We lose authenticity, don't we?

We lose drama, too. Somehow the sense of immediacy has vanished, and we're left with some polite conversation.

Which isn't quite what the author had in mind for this passage.

We don't, of course, always have to use "argot" in order to write a scene with interior dialogue, though we should remember the three keepsakes from Jonathan Swift: keep it lean, keep it under control, keep it purposeful. . .

And now let's add a fourth: *keep it believable*!

Would a character suddenly begin to tell a story with interior dialogue, if he or she hadn't shown an inclination before this? We have to prepare the reader in the sense that the character must be the kind of person who can tell a story within a story and do it well.

Or, alternatively, we must set the scene so the interior dialogue is a necessary part of what is going on. Take a look at Phillip Roth's *The Anatomy Lesson*. Roth's favorite character, Nathan Zuckerman, recalls an afternoon's love-making with a massage technician. She tells him about the time a limousine picked her up while she was waiting for a taxi.

The key is this: Zuckerman is trying to remember every word she said and is doing the telling *into a tape recorder*:

"He drove me and drove me and drove me. I thought I was going to the subway, and then he stopped and he said that I owed him twenty dollars. And I didn't have twenty dollars. And I said, 'Well, I can only write you a check.' And he said, 'How can I know the check is good?' And I said, 'You can call my husband.' That is the last thing I wanted to do, but I was so drunk, and so I didn't know what I was doing..."

The tape recorder makes a difference here. Zuckerman is doing a monologue, and he has no audience but himself to perform for. The tape recorder sucks up all his words, not like another character who may be waiting to speak, and so he can dramatize and develop interior dialogue without fear of interruption. Since Zuckerman is trying to give a complete replay of events, it would be natural for him to recreate the conversation the woman told him she had with the limousine driver.

The interior dialogue comes across as a perfectly appropriate part of the scene. And the tape recorder is a fine piece of stage business.

Still, Roth is careful. He doesn't spend much time with the interior dialogue because he knows its use can be fragile. Like many other dialogue devices, it must be rationed for best results.

The reason? The effectiveness of the underlying dialogue is lost, otherwise.

Jonathan Swift gave us some keepsakes, and if we were to build on them, we might remember that interior dialogue has to be pursued carefully, yet with directness (we can't weasel our way into it), and it must be believable.

It also:

- must not be overused; when in doubt, leave it out;
- must have a purpose, either to develop characterization or to move the plot along;
- must be natural, and consistent with the underlying dialogue.

15

How Do I Handle Questions and Answers?

"...when he swerved across the white line and just missed an oncoming car..." the professor said. He waited while the sixty law students stirred uncomfortably. Incomprehension was general.

He leaned forward, his words clipped. "...about opposite the schoolyard..."

Again, incomprehension.

"C'mon, folks," he urged.

"Give us a clue," a voice from the back said.

The professor waited another moment, then he shrugged. "What course is this?"

"Evidence!" came a small chorus.

He held his palms up, arms apart. "So?"

More incomprehension. Then, from the back, a hand shot up.

The professor nodded.

"Questions," came the reply. "You want questions. Finding evidence is asking good questions."

A smile creased the professor's face. "What were the statements I gave you?"

"Answers."

"So give me the questions," the professor said, and the students did. When they were finished, the professor told them, "The lesson is simple. We've got to ask the right question to get the right answer. If we want the right answer, *be sure to ask the right question.*"

Questions and answers, they do not spin in separate worlds, independent of one another. They work with one another as a team, and when we write dialogue that includes questions and answers, we must be aware, not only why we are using them, but how effective they will be. I'm not referring to one or two questions and answers in the course of other dialogue; this use is fairly easy to control. What we want to look at here are circumstances where the bulk of dialogue in a series of passages is heavily weighted with questions and answers.

Such as in a courtroom or an interrogation.

How do we handle this kind of thing? The key is: *questions and answers must be woven into the fabric of the story so they seem natural and consistent.*

Natural and consistent.

The easiest approach is to understand what dialogue questions and answers must and must not do. They:
  - must propel the plot forward; Robyn Carr says this is so that we "get to know the characters through the way they react to external stimuli";
  - must avoid pointless, extraneous debate;
  - must not be overused; Peggy Simson Curry says too many questions and answers "give the dialogue a lack of forward movement";
  - must not do the job of exposition.

In an earlier chapter we saw Arturo Vivante portray certain questions and answers as "passport dialogue"—"what's your name?"..."where do you live?"...and so forth. His reasoning was that these items simply do not move the story along. They are extraneous to the action and could be summarized much more simply in narration, or in certain cases not even mentioned. We must ask ourselves...are these questions and their answers important to the story? Do they, in Anthony Trollope's words, contribute to the telling of the story?

To write a good story, it's necessary to limit these "passport" questions and answers, as Vivante makes clear, but, if we use them, we have to make sure they will propel the story forward. Yet in the hands of a highly accomplished writer even "passport" questions and answers can work well. See how Frank O'Connor, the Irish short-story writer, does it with his tale, *The Pretender*. Michael and Susie, aged about twelve, brother and sister, are informed by their mother that she's invited Denis, whom they have never met, for dinner. Afterwards, the children are upstairs talking, and Denis stares at the toys Michael and Susie have. Michael is the narrator:

> "Haven't you any toys of your own?" I asked.
> "No," he said.
> "Where do you live?" asked Susie.
> "The Buildings."
> "Is that a nice place?"
> "Tis all right." Everything was "all right" with him.
> Now, I knew The Buildings because I passed it every day on the way to school and I knew it was not all right. It was far from it. It was a low-class sort of place where the kids went barefoot and the women sat all day on the doorsteps talking.
> "Haven't you any brothers and sisters?" Susie went on.
> "No. Only me mudder...and me Aunt Nellie," he added after a moment.
> 'Who's your Aunt Nellie?"
> "My Auntie. She lives down the country. She comes up of an odd time."
> "And where's your daddy?" asked Suzie.
> "What's that?"...

Most of Suzie's questions and Denis's answers are of the "passport" variety, but somehow they work well. The first thing to note is that the characters are children, and as with so many other circumstances, we tend to forgive children for those things we might condemn in their parents. In other words, kids ask a multitude of questions. We expect it, and we're not put off by it. Kids don't have the inhibitions we adults do, so a conversation like this is customary, and entertaining.

Secondly, see how these questions actually do propel the plot. They tell us quite a bit about Denis—where he comes from, that he has no toys, that he lives with his mother and Aunt Nellie. As we get to know Denis, we see the vast difference between him and Michael and Susie, and it is the difference that moves the story along.

There is another thing to be aware of here, too: O'Connor breaks up his questions and answers with a passage of narration, and this serves to change the pace and to underscore some of the information the earlier questions and answers provided. It also prevents the action in the story from growing static, and it injects an ominous note (''a low-class sort of place...kids went barefoot''...) which then can be the springboard for succeeding questions and answers.

All of this in one short passage. But we should be careful because what works with kids often does not work with adults. Put these same questions and answers in the mouths of adults and see the difference.

Boring, we'd say. No movement, no story push.

The classic question-and-answer situation in literature is in the courtroom. The action revolves around questions and answers, and the drama is often supplied by the atmosphere itself. Yet unrelieved questions and answers will eventually lead to boredom, too. So we have to know how to break things up and give the reader a different perspective.

Not much, actually, is required because the courtroom drama is generally intense in and of itself. But for change of pace and to add to characterization, the most appropriate technique is to provide gesturing to the characters.

Why gesturing?

So we can get a better handle on their feelings as they speak.

Let's take a look at the famous court-martial scene from *The Caine Mutiny* by Herman Wouk. Commander Phillip Queeg is on the stand, and he's being questioned about the incident where he dropped a yellow dye marker off the beach at Kwajalein Island as he led a flotilla of invasion boats towards shore. He was supposed to stay with the boats until they made their final run for the beach, but the accusation is that he came about and left the scene early, thus leaving the boats without protection. Queeg is being questioned by Captain Blakely, in charge of the court-martial board:

"From the time you made rendezvous with the boats, Commander, until the time you dropped the marker, what was the widest gap between you and the boats?"

"Well, distances are deceptive over water, particularly with those lowlying boats."

"Did you stay within hailing distance of them?" Blakely said with a slight impatient tone.

"Hailing distance? No. We communicated by semaphore. I might have swamped them if I'd stayed within hailing distance."

Blakely pointed at the red head officer at the far left of the bench. "Lieutenant Murphy informs the court that he was a boat officer in similar situations in these invasions. He says the common practice was to stay within hailing distance, never more than a hundred or a hundred fifty yards apart."

Queeg slumped in his seat, looked out from under his eyebrows at the lieutenant. "Well, that may be. It was a windy day and the bow wave made a lot of wash. It was simpler to semaphore than to go screaming through megaphones."

"Did you have the conn?"

Queeg paused. "As I recall..."

Note the gestures: *Blakely said with a slight impatient tone ...Blakely pointed...Queeg slumped...looked out from under his eyebrows...Queeg paused...*Each of these breaks up the rapid-fire question-and-answer process, but not to the extent that the impact of the dialogue is lost. Instead, we get a small change of pace, coupled with a sense of how the characters are feeling as they say the words. Once we know that Blakely is impatient or that Queeg is slumped in his chair, we can imagine one character's loss of sympathy coinciding with another character's growing defensiveness. The conflict, in other words, becomes heightened, and the drama grows more intense.

Those of us who have spent more than a few moments in a courtroom know the action is often tedious. There isn't much body movement, words themselves are the source of what is happening. So, as writers, we have to make those words become the story. How something is asked and the way it is responded to are the crucial items, and we try to color the questions and answers with characterization:

"What did you do next?" His eyes bore into hers implacably...

"And I suppose you didn't try to stop him?" he said, staring out at the spectators...

"I didn't think he'd understand," she said, massaging her empty ring finger...

Questions and answers with gestures; there are no dead spots now.

One thing we must be careful with is to avoid letting our questions and answers do the job of narration, or exposition. Each question and each answer should be designed to move the story forward. Let's leave major explanations, such as chronicles of family history, lengthy, complicated anecdotes, detailed physical descriptions, arduous journeys, to narration, and concentrate on building tension and character with our dialogue.

Dialogue, in other words, should not be packed with extraneous matter. Questions and answers, useful as they are, are simply a tool for moving the story along. The shorter we keep them, and the more focused, the less likely we will be to slip off the path.

"You think he'll come back for us?"

"That's a dumb question."

If the characterization is clear, no further words are needed to tell us what's going to happen. We demand:
- no lengthy explanations;
- no pointless debates.

We understand.

That's what good questions and answers in dialogue are supposed to accomplish.

16

What About Terms of Art and Slang?

"I guess I better *stump the pew*..." (to pay a debt)
"Lookit 'im, old *gotch-gutted*..." (pot-bellied)
"A real *pea wacker* we're in..." (heavy fog)

Strange words and phrases to us in the twentieth century, relics of another day, arcane reflections of speech patterns that once were in everyday use.

Slang!

Did people really speak this way? Of course they did, but as with many other aspects of the language, the words and phrases people use change and change again as the years go by.

We see it in our lifetimes. Is anyone a *beatnik* these days? Do we still *gild the lily*? How about catching the *milk run*?

When we put words in the mouths of characters, we have to be careful with the colloquialisms we use—slang, in other words. Every period of history has had its peculiar idioms, and we have to know which ones apply to which set of years.

> Raleigh held her close, shielding her from the scaffold construction in the courtyard. "Prithee, dear Lady," he consoled, "the media will cover this hanging well"...

Is *media* a proper word to use with this scene? The media are a product of the second half of the twentieth century, and they don't fit a medieval castle scene. This, obviously, is an extreme example, but it points to the importance of weighing our colloquialisms carefully so we don't have our characters sounding as if they've been asleep for twenty years or more.

And the problem is compounded by the fact that what is slang today may disappear quickly, only to be replaced by something else. What comes into the language also leaves it, and if we put old words in the mouth of a new character, we're liable to have the reader shake his head...*doesn't this writer know anything?*

We lose the respect of the reader, and then we lose the reader. Simple as that.

One thing to watch out for is slang that seems to have blossomed with a heady burst, more on quickness than on longevity. Trendy words and phrases, for example. Here's William Zinsser on the subject:

> The only trouble with accepting words that entered the language overnight is that they have a tendency to leave as abruptly as they came. The 'happenings' of the late 1960s no longer happen, 'out of sight' is out of sight, nobody does his 'thing' anymore, 'relevant' has been hooted out of the room, and where only yesterday we wanted our leaders to have 'charisma', today we want a man who has 'clout'. . .

Slang definitely has a place in dialogue; it's the means by which we reach the reader and encourage his or her sense of identity. We use comfortable, familiar words, we set an informal tone, and then we settle back—reader and writer—and pursue the story together. There is, however, good slang and bad slang, and when we choose our idioms, we must be conscious that what was a character's *cup of tea* thirty years ago might be his *bag* today.

Bad slang can take several forms: it can be offensive, in the sense that any crude word or phrase is offensive; it can be inappropriate, in the sense that it is no longer pertinent; it can be uncharacteristic, in the sense that certain characters would simply not use these idioms; it can be overbearing, in the sense that the word or phrase is used to the point of gagging us, and we want to scream "enough! enough!"

Good slang, though, can inject life and immediacy into a story. It can turn a commonplace tale into high drama. This is what Irwin Faust does with his *The Year of the Hot Jock*, told in the idiom of the thoroughbred jockey, without quotation marks. Pablo is to ride Wineglo in the Preakness, and he runs into his old friend Rafael in the lobby of the hotel:

Listen, he says fast and jerky, don't win.

Stare, open mouth, close, open. Did I hear what I heard?

Don't win, Paul.

Face gets hot, keep voice down. Soft, low: this horse can't miss, Rafe.

Eyes stop shifting gears, voice levels off. You got the hands Paulie, you can do it.

Don't answer, not yet, maybe he exits while he can. Sits there, not going anywhere. He once told me: In this world anything can happen. Think of that, finally, say it. Rafael, you asking me to pull my horse?

I'm asking you not to kill him to win.

You asking me to pull him?

Don't be so damn technical...

The situation is stereotypical—a jockey being asked to prevent his horse from winning—and there are only so many ways this can be presented. Ultimately, the proposal has to be made —*pull the horse, don't let him win*—and the reaction has to be portrayed—*I will (or won't) do as you ask* . . .

But note the style. It reads like a telegram, abbreviated phrases, words running together, everything intensified. The slang phrases are here—*horse can't miss...you got the hands ...not to kill him to win...pull my horse?* . . . What's important is that the slang fits with the general dialogue, and is perfectly appropriate for the mood of the story.

The slang is as natural as the story itself.

Good slang because it blends well.

Doesn't the story benefit from the slang? The immediacy and the drama are right before our eyes. Anything less colloquial would take that away.

Let's substitute—*this horse is the best in the field . . . we want you to lose . . . you know how to do it . . .*

Is it the same?

There's a hollowness in there, a lack of authenticity. That's what good slang is designed to avoid.

Good slang allows us to use familiar colloquialisms, but what about those times when we have unfamiliar words and phrases, and there just isn't an effective substitute? Or when we want to use unfamiliar words and phrases to add to the mood of our story?

We call these "terms of art," and they represent a body of language which must be carefully weighed before being used. We see these terms appear when something of a scientific nature is discussed, or something medical or something artistic . . . anything, in fact, which has developed its own language so that a non-member of the group would be at a loss to understand. Suppose, for example, we're in a courtroom, and the opposing lawyers are discussing a point of law before the Bench:

"I think it's appropriate to bring in *res ipsa loquitur*, Your Honor. . ."

"Not unless the *Parole Evidence Rule* has been repealed. There's no way we're going to impeach our *extrajudicial* testimony. . ."

"Gentlemen," the Judge reminded them, "this is not a *Court of Equity* . . ."

The italicized words, of course, are terms of art, the lawyer's art, but under different circumstances they could be the physicist's art, the trumpet player's art, the advertising man's art, and so forth. The point is that whenever we have a character with a specialty, and the action revolves around that specialty, we have to know when to use the specialty's terms of art, and whether to explain such words and phrases to a quizzical reader. It's the same judgment we make with bad slang: if we lose the reader's respect with bad slang, we cause the reader to become confused with esoteric terms of art. In either case, the result is the same:

We lose the reader.

Terms of art, then, must be carefully offered. The first and most important thing to remember is never to overdo it. When in doubt, cut back on the terms of art, keeping them around only to propel the story forward.

And, if possible, provide some form of explanation, or at least offer reasons why the terms of art are relevant.

See how Edward Stewart does it in his book, *Ballerina*, the story of young ballet dancers in an international ballet company in New York. Chris, one of the dancers, is to work on a new ballet with Wally Collins, a highly respected male dancer. Marius Vollmar, the ballet master, is to rehearse them:

> Vollmar let the music continue to the end. He thanked the pianist, got to his feet and began pacing, waving his arms.
>
> "Music is our staircase. This is simple music; it makes a simple staircase. No spirals, no zigzags, no drooping over the banister. We go up, we come down again. We have two tempos: the *andante*, the *piu mosso*. They are repeated. Same stairs up, same stairs down. Wally—where is our emotional climax? Where are the stairs steepest?"
>
> "The last *allegro*."
>
> "Christine?"
>
> She hesitated to disagree with her partner, but. . . "The second *andante*."
>
> "What phrase in the second *andante*?"
>
> "The two silences. . ."

Andante...allegro...piu mosso... there is no attempt to define or explain these musical terms, yet they are essential to the ballet the characters will learn. Would someone without musical training understand them? Or, more importantly, does a failure to understand them affect an understanding of the plot?

Probably not. We know several things from this passage: the characters are learning a new ballet, and they must learn the music that goes with it; Chris and Wally disagree about the location of the emotional climax; the music has an "up tempo" and a "down tempo," and these are the only tempos and it is simple music.

We also get some implied explanation of the terms of art; note Vollmar's description of the music—a "simple staircase." Don't we "hear" how it sounds, can't we imagine the dancers moving to this music?

And isn't this all we need to know to keep up with the plot? The terms of art add a certain mood to the scene, but for us who have no musical background, it's enough to know the general trend of the music and to see that Chris picks up its subtleties more easily than Wally.

The point is this: unless it is necessary for an understanding of the story, detailed explanations of terms of art are not necessary. We can imply meanings, if we wish, but even this should be done only when we wish to nudge the plot along.

There are times, though, when we must add an explanation to the unfamiliar terms we use. We should ask ourselves: would *I* be confused if I didn't get an explanation? This is especially true where several terms of art appear within a short space; some, at least, should be explained, so that the reader can get the drift of what is happening.

In Gerald Green's *The Hostage Heart*, we see an example of explanation and non-explanation, but there's little doubt about what's happening. In this passage Dr. Eric Lake is about to operate on Walter Trench for a coronary by-pass:

Dr. Lake put his scalpel at a point on Trench's aorta about one inch above the heart. "Right here for the graft to the LAD," he said. He moved the scalpel up an inch. "And here for the graft to the diagonal. How does that look, Jack?"

"Looks fine, Eric."

Mihrab nodded. Lake would put the grafts where he wanted. But he always included the junior surgeons in his decisions.

"There's an artery that's really shot," Lake said. He touched the wider end with his gloved fingers. "Beading. A good part of the way down. Just a matter of time before it closed off. Feel it, Jack." *Beading* described the bits of hardness in a vessel grown narrow, obstructing the flow of blood...

Green does not explain his reference to LAD, but he does give us a full explanation for "beading." What's the difference? It's probably a case of not letting too many terms of art go on without remembering the reader. Then, too, "beading" is a condition that affects the particular patient's health, a key symptom; LAD refers to a piece of tissue, something common in all of us. "Beading" is special, different, uncommon, LAD is none of these things.

So we get an explanation of the less familiar term of art. And it doesn't interrupt the flow of the story, does it? In fact, by understanding "beading," we feel a greater sense of immediacy:

- The condition is serious!
- The man might die!
- Thank God, we operated in time!

"Terms of art should be sprinkled delicately," says the writer...

"Terms of art help me to understand," says the reader...

And slang brings us together.

17

What If I Want to Get a Few Laughs?

"I'd like to be funny," said Alice.

"Chop down fifty trees in the forest," responded the King of Hearts, patting his ample belly.

"Would that make me funny?"

"Oh no, of course not."

"*You* are not funny!"

"Why would I want to be funny?"

"I'm the one who wants to be funny," said Alice with a frown.

"See! Already you are becoming funny."

"I'm serious!" Alice stamped her foot.

"Of course," smiled the king...

Humor writing is broadly represented in our literature, and we can use it to make a variety of points, from criticism to adulation. In this refitted segment from Lewis Carroll's story about Alice in Wonderland, there is a point: *humor is serious business; in order to write funny, we have to be unfunny.*

No, not a misstatement.

- *William Zinsser*: "...if you're trying to write humor, almost everything that you do is serious."

- *E.B. White*: Humor ". . . need only speak the truth—
and I notice it always does."

When the King tells Alice to chop down trees in the forest,
he's saying that if she wants to be funny, she should learn how
to be serious. What better way to learn seriousness than to be
burdened with chopping down trees? When Alice feels frustration and stamps her foot, the first stirrings of seriousness appear.
When she admits to becoming serious, the King is satisfied.
Now, she can be funny.

Humor comes in many forms—imitation, mockery, nonsense,
incongruity. They all depend on a receptive audience and a
serious-minded writer, and what they try to do, all of them, is to
take an average, normal happening or circumstance and flip
it—make it at least one beat off—so it sparks a laugh or a
chuckle.

Dialogue, it's safe to say, is one of the most useful devices for
developing and presenting humor, especially with fiction.
Someone can *say* something funny much more quickly and easily than a passage of narrative can describe it. Also, as we've
seen, dialogue gives us that sense of immediacy and drama that
allows the spoken word to explode on our reading consciousness.
We are caught up in the scene, and we can appreciate the
humor easily.

See, for example, how Donald Westlake handles humor in
this scene from his book, *High Adventure*. The story is set in
Belize, Central America, and it concerns artifact hunting and
smuggling. In the passage below, Whitman Lemuel, an antiques expert and museum curator, is seated in a large hotel dining room across from two gay New York antiques dealers,
Witcher and Feldspan, who are trying to smuggle antiquities
out of the country. Somehow, Witcher and Feldspan have the
idea Lemuel is a drug dealer instead of the harmless, self-
important character he really is, and Lemuel is watching someone else in the dining room whom he believes is out to get
him . . .

In his nervousness, Lemuel crunched duckling bones, eating the wings entire.

"He's eating *bones*," Feldspan said.

"Gerry, stop *looking* at him."

Feldspan blinked. He wanted Witcher's Gibson, but Witcher kept holding it. He said, "He looks like Meyer Lansky."

"He does not," Witcher said, though he didn't turn around to look. "Meyer Lansky was about a hundred, and Jewish."

"He could be Jewish."

"Gerry."

"Meyer Lansky wasn't always a hundred. It's just like *The Godfather*; they almost look like normal people, but they have dead eyes. It's because their souls are black"...

Two classic humor techniques are revealed here: mistaken identity and exaggeration. Neither would work so well alone, but together they bring a smile. If we had only mistaken identity, and the menacing character Lemuel was thought to be was someone whose name wouldn't ring with instant recognition, is there humor? Not much, certainly. And if the exaggeration relates to the self-important Lemuel, not as a drug dealer, but as something less menacing, there is little room for humor.

But put them together, a bigger-than-life sinister character with seemingly murderous designs, and the image is humorous, especially when we know that Lemuel is anything but a Mafia type. That, in fact, is the key to why this is so funny...Lemuel is a silly little man, and the thought of his portraying a Mafia leader is so ridiculous as to be laughable...

Which is the point, of course.

Had the author depended upon narrative technique here, he would have had a more difficult time showing the humor in this scene, the gross exaggerations and distortions, the overreactions and panic explosions, with the dramatic effect that the dialogue has produced. The humor is in what the characters say, in how they react.

Some people have tried to categorize humor, as if in doing so, special insights into the writing of it can be achieved. Perhaps this has some application when working with plot or characterization, but insofar as dialogue is concerned, it matters little what type of humor we want to portray. Parody or satire, nonsense or burlesque, the dialogue must still be sharp and pointed...and *believable*!

That is, we must see it as humor.

"On the whole," said E.B. White, many years ago, "the humorists who contribute pleasure to a wide audience are the ones who create characters and tell tales, the ones who are story tellers at heart."

Story tellers.

If we're not adept at telling a story, then we won't be adept at creating humor. But if we can tell a story, it remains a story no matter the humor category. So the same dialogue rules that apply to other forms of writing apply to humor, also. Dialogue that moves the plot, dialogue that develops characterization, dialogue that sets the mood and so forth, even if done humorously, must still meet the standards we have already explored in earlier chapters.

Yet there are some specifics we ought to be aware of even with humorous-dialogue writing. All but one could probably be applied equally to most non-humorous writing forms, but they should be emphasized here, in any case.

- Humor does not need a lead-in. (This is the one that most applies to humor dialogue; it means we don't write "Now for a funny story..." If it's funny, the reader will get it from the portrayal.)
- The humor should be controlled. (Don't overdo the portrayal, don't let it run on and on and on and on...)
- Allow the reader's imagination to flower. (Every detail,

every aspect, need not be set out; humor thrives more from suggestion than from declaration.)

- When in doubt, think dialogue. It's the best way to get humor across.

"Humor," wrote Mark Twain, "is only a fragrance, a decoration. Often it is merely an odd trick of speech and spelling. . . ."
Is the old master correct?

Take a look at this passage from *Confessions of a Galloman-iac*, by Frank Moore Colby. The author decided he would learn French, and he sought out those who spoke the language. He met a Frenchman whose English matched Colby's French, and they agreed to interchange their languages, the author talking in French and the Frenchman talking in English. They met daily for two weeks and walked for an hour in the park. The author recalls a typical conversation:

"It calls to walk," said he brilliantly.

"It is good morning," said I, "better than I had extended."

"I was at you yestairday ze morning, but I deed not find."

"I was obliged to leap early," said I, "and I thank, but positively are you not deranged?"

"Don't talk," said I. "Never talk again. It was really nothing anywhere. I had been very happy, I reassure". . .

The humor reflects what Twain was talking about. *An odd trick of speech or spelling* . . . makes us chuckle because the conversation is so ludicrous. Each knows just enough about the other's language to say silly things in a silly manner. The effects of a little knowledge are exaggerated to the point where they become funny.

Because the author and his friend are trying to be serious. Colby doesn't portray them as setting out to do something funny, nor does he say to us as an aside . . . watch this! What a laugh!

Each man is trying to learn the other's language, and the passage shows us what happens when the speaker doesn't understand the words he is using.

The results are utter nonsense.

And *that's* funny.

By far the most intellectually demanding of the forms of humor are parodies and satire. They are appreciated by a relatively small audience, so any writing done in these areas must be sharply pointed and clearly done. Broad humor, for example, would not work here; clownish actions and dialogue, slapstick, and foolish pratfalls deflect the point of the story.

E.B. White feels that almost all humor can be satire, and in a broad sense he's probably correct. If we define satire as a series of comments—sometimes savagely written—designed to point out flaws or contradictions or unattractive human characteristics or just human weirdness, we could cover almost anything. To satirize something is to portray it with wit yet not allow ourselves to descend to guffaws.

The chuckle, the wry smile, are what satire is intended to produce.

Parodies are designed to spoof something or someone, usually by exaggerating those things we wish to comment on. Suppose we want to skewer the wholesomeness of holier-than-thou Sunday school outings? Donald Stewart begins his story, *The Whiskey Rebellion*, this way:

> "Just the *day* for a Whiskey Rebellion," said Aunt Polly and off they ran, lipperty-lipperty-lip to get a few shooting rifles.
>
> "Oh goody goody," cried little Emily. "Now we can all shoot at those horrid Revenue Officers..."

Good parody, E.B. White goes on, "should be funny in itself, whether or not one has read the book or author parodied." He feels that what are necessary are a good ear and an appreciation of the audience.

And in this sense both parody and satire work the same way. To do it right, we...

- must have a thorough understanding of our subject;
- must recognize that the audience will be educated and intelligent.

So...our dialogue must be carefully drawn to reflect the nature of those we're writing for.

Educated and intelligent.

But there are many other humor forms, some of them much more fun to read than a parody or satire. This book certainly wouldn't be complete without a contribution from the writer who gave us the book title. Here's Ring Lardner's story, *Sit Still*, about a man hailing and riding in a taxi. The reference to Mr. Schwartz means absolutely nothing:

"Where were you headed for?" I retorted.

"Nowhere special," he said.

"Well," I said, "I figured we might as well ride together as long as we were headed in the same direction. How did Mr. Schwartz come to send you one of his pictures? Do you know him?"

"I'm one of his fans," said the driver. "What I'd appreciate now, though, is where you want me to take you."

"You'll be one of the first people I'll tell as soon as I find out. Just drive along a ways and if I hear anything, I'll get in touch with you."

"All right," said the driver, "and maybe you'd better rap twice on the window so I'll know it's you. That will be the signal. Have you got it?"

"Two raps," I said.

"You pick things up quickly, but whether you remember them is the question. Perhaps it will help if you connect it in your mind with some common fact like how many legs on a man, or how many rear wheels on a car."

"Or how many times I've been abroad," I chuckled...

This is pure nonsense, simply a series of absurd dialogue lines which will lead to an absurd ending. Why is it funny?

Because it sounds reasonable, though it really isn't. It's exaggeration to an implausible degree.

As we picture the conversation in our mind, the characters seem to be making sense only to themselves.

To us it's nonsense.

And nonsense can be funny.

18

How Do I Foreshadow Future Events?

It is Act I, Scene 2, of Shakespeare's *Julius Caesar*. Caesar and Mark Antony enter the public square and note Brutus and Cassius in quiet conversation. Caesar remarks that he would prefer docile, well-fed men as his supporters. Then he says:

"Yon Cassius has a lean and hungry look; He thinks too much, such men are dangerous..."

And of course he is right. Before the play is ended, Caesar has been assassinated by Brutus who was urged on by Cassius in a wide-ranging plot to remove Caesar from the throne.

Cassius is dangerous, indeed!

And we, the readers, learn of Caesar's suspicions early so we can keep watch and see if they are well founded. What we are given is a hint of something to come later.

A hint.

That's foreshadowing. It's a technique or device to provide an early motivation for something to come later.

Why do we need foreshadowing? One reason, according to Lawrence Block, is so "the writer prepares the reader for a sharp turn in the plot, without tipping his hand altogether." Another way of saying this is that the reader won't feel jerked around when the unexpected event or events take place.

An additional reason is to build suspense. Dialogue works here easily. Consider the following:

"I never forget a face"...

"I don't like the look of those clouds over there"...

"I'd die if you ever left me"...

"I'm sure we've never met"...

Each of these implies something more, and we'll only find out if we continue with the story. For example, "I never forget a face"...implies that something happened—something sinister, perhaps—which etched the face in the memory. The speaker may be having difficulty now in remembering, but what about the future? If he remembers, what will that do to the story? What, in fact, might he remember, and once having remembered, what further might he do about it?

The writer gives us a hint now, and if we stay with the story, we'll receive the entire package later. We wonder, we guess, we grow concerned—all the elements that make up suspense. From a simple passage of dialogue we are caught up in the web of the story, and somewhere, we know, the story will be influenced by the hint we received.

Foreshadowing can be applied to many situations. It is a device, after all, which influences a variety of plot lines, from stories of romance to stories of courage, from stories of horror to stories of beauty and grace. It is most often used to reflect the promise of heightened tension—that is, we are offered the hint of greater conflict to come at some point in the future. Danger, disaster, severe agony will accompany this use of foreshadowing, and it's apparent that the storyline, in order to accommodate these severe consequences, will zig and zag.

Thus, we go back to Lawrence Block: foreshadowing "prepares the reader for a sharp turn in the plot..." and we know that means any plot, any turn.

There is one general limitation: foreshadowing should *not* be used repeatedly in a story. An occasional use is better, just as an occasional drift into dialect or an occasional gesture provides sufficient uplift to a passage of dialogue. Too much foreshadowing will confuse the reader because the plot will maneuver like a jack rabbit on the run. It's best to foreshadow only when we want to pique the reader's interest about a future event or circumstance, and we want to lay the groundwork now. It should *not* be used when the tension of the moment is already high, nor should it be used when the event to be foreshadowed is not of great importance to the storyline.

Foreshadowing, in other words, has only limited purpose and application. It is not a substitute for the action, itself, and it must offer enough so that the reader will take notice and be impressed.

The way foreshadowing is applied becomes the key to its use. Generally, it has three distinct approaches:
- blatant, straightforward;
- as a teaser;
- in an overstated manner.

The blatant approach is certainly the easiest to use, and it's quite common. See how Rosellen Brown deals with it in her novel, *Tender Mercies*. Dan and Laura are married and Laura is a recent quadraplegic because of a boating accident, where Dan was at the wheel. Dan is hiring a nurse for Laura who is confined to the upstairs bedroom. The nurse, who has been on duty for only two days, comes downstairs and confronts Dan:

"I cannot work with her if she tells me how to go about my business," the nurse says. "Patients are notoriously sure they know what is best for themselves when they are in fact often the last ones to know."

"Well, what kind of problems are you having? As far as I can see your business is her comfort. Isn't it?" He asks himself; double checks. Surely it isn't the nurse's comfort that's at stake. He wishes they had hired a friend.

"Then I think you'll understand if I say this is a situation that is not—is *not*—going to work out to my satisfaction. As a professional, this is. Your wife is a perfectly nice young woman but she is going to make no progress with her infirmity if she doesn't take herself in hand. Certain things are clear as glass and this is one of them''...

What's being foreshadowed here? On one level it's the conflict between Laura and the nurse, but on another level it's the situation of a quadraplegic attempting to control what's being done to her. As we read, we get the feeling that the situation remains barely manageable, and that at some point it may actually become chaotic.

How do we sense this? By the nurse's adamant stand, by Dan's reflexive response to his wife's discomfort, and by the nurse finally saying that the situation is impossible. Note her words: *this is a situation that is not—is not—going to work out.* This is foreshadowing in the most direct way. We are told, blatantly, that there are problems with the care of the patient, and we are left to imagine how pervasive they can be. We are not witnesses to the scene between the nurse and Laura, so we don't know exactly what was said, but the nurse's tight-lipped response can only spell trouble for her successor.

And that's the true essence of foreshadowing. We, the readers, can now say to ourselves, *So! A problem here. Let's remember*...Then, as the story unwinds, we can observe the problem surfacing again and again. We don't feel cheated or confused, because we were alerted to it.

The nurse's words, of course, are much more than a hint of something to come. They spell out the dimensions of the difficulty—that Laura is an unwieldy patient and will not do as she is told—and then in succeeding scenes, we discover the specific reasons she has for acting this way, and the specific actions she will take to confront the problem.

The foreshadowing is clear and unambiguous. There is no attempt to soften it or obfuscate it.

Another approach to foreshadowing, however, is not as blatant in its presentation. This is where the hint of future action is most appropriate, where the foreshadowing comes off as a "teaser" or "tickler" of something that will happen later. Subtlety is important because we don't want to overemphasize what is being said.

For example, in the above passage from *Tender Mercies*, suppose we have the nurse saying in response to Dan's question about her problems with Laura:

"We're going to try very hard. It's not easy, you know..."

This is not as blatant as the response in the book, yet we get a flavor of the same situation. It's more like a hint, but we know there could be trouble down the line.

The "teaser" effect builds tension and suspense more delicately than the blatant approach, allowing not just one but several hints to fall before the entire effect becomes known.

See how Michael Gilbert does it with his story, *The Danger Within*, about prisoners at a World War II German prison camp planning a mass escape. One of the prisoners had been moved to a cell and was about to be hanged, but was freed at the last moment because of the death of Mussolini. He is returned to the prisoners' barracks where he is questioned by the other prisoners:

"Was there anything else you picked up that might be useful?"

"Well—no. Nothing in particular." For a moment Byfold looked almost embarrassed.

"Certain?"

"Yes, quite certain. If I do think of anything, I'll let you know."

At this point we have a hint that perhaps he did, in fact, hear something. But he doesn't think it important enough to divulge.

A few moments later, he is questioned again:

"Did you pick up anything else that might be useful while you were over the other side?"

"No sir. Nothing startling."

If there was, once again, a certain hesitancy in Byfold's manner, Colonel Lavery apparently didn't notice it . . .

Later, Byfold confides that he thought he heard someone speaking English, and this, of course, means there is a traitor in their midst. In Lawrence Block's words, the uncovering of this information is the sharp plot-turn, and the hints concerning it come from Byfold's lips. Note that Byfold never actually says anything to confirm this; the hints we get come from his slight uncertainties, which he then quickly covers up. These uncertainties are "teasers," mentioned earlier, and their appearance is enough to make us scratch our heads . . . why isn't he so sure, we ask ourselves. What happened? . . . Then, later, when the truth is uncovered, we feel comfortable that we knew *something* wasn't right.

The other side of the "teaser" approach is to make our foreshadowing so overstated that we engender an opposite reaction. In other words, we don't foreshadow in a blatant manner, we do it overwhelmingly, tipping the scales so far in one direction that any thoughtful reader has to smile and say . . . the author means us to go in the opposite direction!

Overstatement to this degree isn't the sole province of foreshadowing. It's a device that can be used to encourage any type of response in any type of relationship. For example, a woman going on and on about how she dislikes a certain man can make us wonder if, in Shakespeare's words, she "doth protest too much." Overstatement is a valuable tool, and it works with foreshadowing. Note how Vladimir Nabokov uses it in his short novel, *The Enchanter*. This book is really a forerunner of his work, *Lolita*, and in it he has his narrator mad for a nubile young girl who happens to be the daughter of a sickly, overbearing mother. The narrator cozies up to the mother and convinces her they should marry, so the narrator can have the young girl within easy reach. The girl, however, has been living with the mother's friends, and the narrator now tries to show the mother why the girl should move in with them after they marry. The mother remains unmoved.

"Of course you can do as you please," he said nervous- ly, frightened by her silence (he had gone too far!).

"I've already told you," she drawled with that same ridiculous martyr-like softness, "That what is paramount to me is my peace and quiet. If it is disrupted I shall die... Listen: there she goes scraping her foot on the floor or banging something—it wasn't very loud, was it?—yet it's already enough to give me a nervous spasm and make me see spots before my eyes. And a child cannot live without banging around; even if there are twenty-five rooms all twenty-five will be noisy. Therefore you'll have to choose between me and her."

"No, no—don't even say such things!" he cried with a panicky catch in his throat. "There isn't even any question of choosing... Heaven forbid! It was just a theoretical con- sideration..."

See how the narrator overworks his reaction to the mother's determination to keep the young girl away: *No, no!...He cried ...a panicky catch in his throat...no question of choosing... Heaven forbid!...* These words and phrases are melodramatic; they are overstatements of his determination not to rock the boat. He has miscalculated. The mother is not yet ready to have the girl in the house, so he must blunt any suspicions she might have. How does he do this? By melodramatic posturing.

Yet we know, don't we, that the narrator has no intention of giving up his quest? We know it because his response signified overreaction, and the question we, as readers, have to ask ourselves is why he should overreact unless he has other motives.

Thus there's more to the overstatement than appears. The words say one thing, but taken together their meaning is some- thing else. That's the key to using overstatement: look at the words together, in total, say them out loud, and they should imply the opposite of what they seem to say.

The foreshadowing, then, tells us that the narrator has no intention of going along with the mother's wishes, but that for the moment he will accede to these wishes because the situation is too tenuous. He has no intention of giving up his demon urge for the young girl, but he certainly doesn't want the mother to know that.

So Nabokov overstates the response, and we realize that the narrator will live to funnel his desires to another day.

"It's all in how you look at it," says the writer.

"So long as you keep the hints coming," says the reader.

19

Suppose I Open With Dialogue? Suppose I Close?

The lead.

The end.

So much goes on in a story after the lead and before the end that we might forget how crucial the opening and the closing really are.

The way we open a story sets the story tone.

The way we close a story provides the final impression the reader takes away.

Crucial. Key. Decisive.

Journalists speak of the lead as the most important sentence in an entire work, and fiction writers talk about endings in terms of satisfying the reader. In both instances the inherent quality of a piece of writing is being held up to scrutiny, and a standard is being set. Does the lead set the tone. . .does the end fulfill most expectations?

As writers we strive to answer with a resounding yes!

But sometimes—the cliché goes—it ain't so easy.

Dialogue, however, is a tool that can help. Because of the sense of immediacy it carries and because it can pack a lot of drama in just a few lines, dialogue can do the job that many more lines of narrative might struggle with.

"It has to be an albino skunk!" Helen said to her pouting mother from the verandah step.

"Can't be," said her brother, Harley Hanscomb. "Circus claimed it was a West African tree squirrel."

"I don't see why you won't move back home for a little while," said their mother to Helen. "How can working in a circus be good for you?"

"You can see the stripe marks down his back," said Helen. . .

In a few short lines we have moved right into this story, we get the tension between Helen and her mother, we find out Helen works for a circus, we learn she has a brother. Would we like to read on?

That, of course, is the point. An opening that doesn't encourage us to read further doesn't make for much of a story. And an ending that doesn't leave us with satisfaction doesn't do its job. While there aren't exact rules on how all of this is done, there are two general principles we should remember:

Openings must be attention-catching.

Closings must provide a slight surprise.

In our lead, if we hook the reader, we have him or her for at least the next few paragraphs, where we must continue the process of imbedding the hook.

In our endings, we want the reader to walk away thinking how it all came out wasn't quite what was expected. Not a huge twist, mind, but something a bit different yet perfectly reasonable. Why a surprise at this point? Remember, the ending is the final impression the reader takes away, and wouldn't we want him or her to feel that the story has to be followed to the end, that stopping before that reduces the pleasure? We want that reading pleasure to be paramount, and therefore we continue to develop the story to the end, so the pleasure is maintained.

Let's go back to openings. In J.F. Powers's story, *The Valiant Woman*, we have three people seated around the dinner table:

two priests and the rectory housekeeper. Remembering that we want to catch the reader's attention rapidly and hold it, watch how Powers begins:

> They had come to the dessert in a dinner that was a shambles. "Well John," Father Nulty said, turning away from Mrs. Stone and to Father Firman, long gone silent at his own table. "You've got the bishop coming for confirmation next week."
>
> "Yes," Mrs. Stone cut in, "and for dinner. And if he don't eat anymore than he did last year—"
>
> Father Firman, in a rare moment, faced it. "Mrs. Stone, the bishop is not well. You know that."
>
> "And after I fixed that fine dinner and all." Mrs. Stone pouted in Father Nulty's direction. . .

The tension is palpable. Mrs. Stone is complaining and the priests are defending. There's disagreement and dissatisfaction, and we'd like to know more. Why is the bishop coming, will Mrs. Stone continue to complain, will the priests finally exert authority over her and stop the complaining, will the complaining lead to other difficulties, how can the priests co-exist with Mrs. Stone? What we have here is *quick* tension, and the reader should be hooked by the second dialogue passage.

There are other ways to catch the reader's attention, though tension-filled dialogue is certainly the quickest and easiest. But note how Ray Bradbury accomplishes it with his story, *The Veldt*. George and Lydia Hadley are living in some indefinite time in the future, and in their home they have a large room they call the "nursery." The story opens:

> "George, I wish you'd look at the nursery."
>
> "What's wrong with it?"
>
> "I don't know."
>
> "Well, then."
>
> "I just want you to look at it, is all, or call a psychologist in to look at it."
>
> "What would a psychologist want with a nursery?"

"You know very well what he'd want." His wife paused in the middle of the kitchen and watched the stove busy humming to itself, making supper for four.

"It's just that the nursery is different now than it was."

"All right, let's have a look" . . .

Is all of this attention-catching? Could we stop reading after the first few lines? Would we *want* to?

Bradbury uses at least three techniques to hook us:

- Questions and answers. There's inherent tension in this approach; it's almost always adversarial.
- Bizarre circumstances. Who ever heard of an inanimate object like a nursery needing a psychologist?
- Unexplained change. The nursery is "different" from what it was; why? what happened? and even more important, what's *going* to happen?

The dialogue here catches us a bit off balance because it's a quiet, seemingly innocuous conversation between husband and wife; it's only when we focus on what they are saying that we realize something weird is going on. That weirdness is what imbeds the hook and pulls the reader along with the story. Most writers know that hooking the reader is a delicate art, and it must be accomplished within a few paragraphs, at most. Bradbury does it here with consummate skill, maintaining, at the same time, the forward pace of the story and the first touches of characterization.

Would we want to read on?

Sure enough.

When we come to endings, the key element remains to provide a small surprise for the reader. It must be logical, of course, and it must be satisfying—no hanging threads of the story should be left untended. But surprise is what makes the story ending memorable.

This is what William Wharton did with his highly acclaimed novel, *Birdy*. Al and Birdy are boyhood friends, and they both find themselves under treatment in a U.S. Army psychiatric hospital during World War II. Birdy has had obsessive boyhood fantasies about becoming a canary, and he dreams of flying off into freedom. They are treated by the hospital psychiatrist, and as the last scene begins the fantasies return. Birdy sees himself with Al standing on the hospital roof throwing baseballs at the sky. The psychiatrist appears and slowly sheds his skin, becoming a golden duckling and urging the young men to follow him into the sky. Al speaks:

"Not me, Birdy. I'm not even going near the edge. I'm not going to jump off a building and get myself killed."

"I'm not either, Al."

"Well, we take the suit that Weiss molted and we put it in the box with what're left of the moldy baseballs. We go back downstairs and check the box at the entrance. Then we walk right on out of here, out the gates."

"Just like that?"

"Just like that."

"And so what happens, then?"

"Nothing, Al, just the rest of our lives."

"Is that all?"

"That's all."

"And that's the way it ends?"

"Not really, Al. It's never that easy. Nobody gets off that easy."

But it's worth trying.

The end. The surprise is this...although Birdy's obsession was to fly like a bird, in this, his final fantasy, he reaches for freedom by walking. The question we're left with is: does this mean Birdy is cured? The answer, of course, is more elusive, and Wharton, like any good writer, allows us to fashion a final scenario for ourselves. But whatever we come up with, it's clear that the final dialogue passage does not interfere with the logical progression of the story, nor leave us wondering and waiting for more. The ending is satisfying because it concludes the fantasy and with it the obsession...perhaps.

Notice that this is a surprise only in the sense that one would expect Birdy and Al to fly after the psychiatrist, given the obsession that Birdy holds. But the fact that they choose to walk out the gate is not so unexpected nor so vast a change. It is, after all, the goal of any psychiatric hospital to try to make the patients whole, and Birdy and Al have been undergoing treatment for an extended period. Now, all of a sudden, they seem cured—at least in the fantasy.

Surprise!

Sometimes we can couple tension with modest surprise and bring about an even more satisfying ending. A disagreement, say, or a confrontation, or a discovery can be portrayed with tension, and at the last moment a surprise can enter and provide a turn-table effect so the characters must readjust immediately.

Remember, though, we must make it logical and satisfying.

See how James McKimmey does it with his mystery-suspense story, *A Proper Environment*. Ambleton killed his wife, and Harms, a household servant, discovered it and agreed to cover up the killing so long as Ambleton paid him money every year. Harms was a huge man, who enjoyed killing and tearing wild animals apart. Harms left Ambleton's employ, and every year the money was paid as promised. One day Ambleton's son, Kevin, overhears his father and Harms on the telephone talking about the murder. Kevin, an avid collector of magic tricks, puts disappearing ink into the inkwell of his father's desk, knowing the next delivery of money to Harms would be addressed with this ink. Later, Kevin confronts his father about murdering his mother:

"Killer," Kevin said.

"If you'd only been old enough to know what she really was."

"You didn't give me the chance," Kevin said cooly.

Behind Kevin, as he spoke, Edward Harms appeared in the doorway, looking much as he had the day seven years before when the boy had been asleep in his room.

"No!" Ambleton told him. "No no no no no!"...

This is the tension of confrontation—between father and son—and some way has to be found to resolve it. The story simply cannot end with father and son glaring at one another and throwing epithets about.

Enter Edward Harms. We know he's vicious and brutal, and we know what he intends to do. This will resolve the confrontation, certainly, and it will also provide a nice, logical, satisfying end to the story. There's surprise, too, in the sense that Harms's entry at this moment may not have been anticipated. But he has motivation to be in the house (because he didn't receive his money, since the ink on the package had disappeared), and the father, who had prevailed through the years by paying blackmail and covering up a murder, was now to be killed. Simple justice, after all.

The ending works, doesn't it? And it has the elements we've discussed: surprise, logic and satisfaction.

The most effective type of surprise for our endings comes in the form of a reversal of what we've come to expect. That is, things go along in one direction, and then, in the end, things get reversed. We mentioned the "turn-table" effect, and this is really only an extension. But it's effective and it's common.

See how D.H. Lawrence uses it in his story, *The Captain's Doll*, about a romantic triangle involving a refugee German baroness and an English Army captain and his wife. The baroness makes dolls. She created one of the Captain which both he and she cherished. Finally, the romance ends, and the Englishman and his wife return to England, while the baroness continues to live on the continent. Years pass, the wife dies, and the Englishman finally locates the baroness in Salzburg, Austria. They reunite and, during a quiet boat ride, discuss whether they should marry. The baroness says she will marry him, but she won't promise to honor and obey him. The Englishman says in that case the marriage will never take place. The boat comes to a stop at the dock of the baroness's villa.

"You'll come in?"

"No, I'll row straight back."

"But you won't have me even if I love you?" she asked him.

"You must promise the other," he said, "it comes in the Marriage Service."

"Don't be a solemn ass. Do come in."

"No," he said, "I don't want to come in."

"Do you want to go away tomorrow? Go, if you do. But anyway I won't say it before the marriage service. I needn't need I?"

She stepped from the boat.

"And come to me tomorrow, will you?" she said.

"Yes, in the morning."

He pulled quietly into the dark...

In the end, she agrees to the Marriage Service and to including the words "honor and obey." It is a reversal of her long-standing point of view, and since it comes at the end of the story, it is surprising. But there's motivation: she does love him, and she wants to be with him. If this is the only way it will happen, she will go along...reluctantly. But note something else. In the earlier years the baroness had her English Captain doll, and it was satisfying for her. She made the doll and she controlled it. Now, suddenly, she has become *his* doll. "Honor and obey" put her in this position, and the roles have been subtly but definitely reversed.

This is Lawrence at his best, and we can appreciate how deftly he maneuvers his characters. But what of the ending? Is it logical, is it satisfying?

An old love offers an aging beauty security and deep feeling. All she has to do is say a couple of words.

The baroness gets what she wants. The English Captain gets what he wants.

We, the readers, get what we want—a story we'll remember.

20

Should I Be Aware of the Rhythm of My Dialogue?

Here's a famous passage from a famous story:

> ..."The cannonading has got the wind up in young Raleigh, sir," said the sergeant. Captain Mitty looked up at him through tousled hair. "Get him to bed," he said wearily. "With the others. I'll fly alone." "But you can't sir," said the sergeant anxiously. "It takes two men to handle that bomber and the Archies are pounding hell out of the air. Von Richtman's circus is between here and Saulier." "Somebody's got to get that ammunition dump," said Mitty. "I'm going over. Spot of brandy?"...

What makes this story memorable? Is the dialogue unusual, does it create unforgettable images in our mind? Are we overwhelmed with wordsmanship?

The simple truth is that this passage flows smooth as silk; there is nothing magic in the dialogue, other than its leanness and its rich tone. We can believe what the characters are saying because it *seems* so real, yet we also understand how unreal it all is. This, of course, is *The Secret Life of Walter Mitty*, by James Thurber, and what we see here is plain fantasy.

And it holds together so well! No awkward phrasing, no uncertain cadence, no abrupt changes of pace or tempo.

The rhythm works!

Every story has to be concerned with rhythm. It is to the writer what time is to the musician and angles are to the sculptor. It is the way a story moves, the way its audience is caught up.

Bad rhythm causes us to sense something out of place, something distasteful. The only reason we would ever use bad rhythm is when we *want* to create the desired effect in the reader. But to use bad rhythm we have to know why it's bad and when it's bad.

For example, we could have a character say:

"What in the world are you doing?"

The rhythm is clean, the tempo even. It's a simple phrase, simply said.

But suppose, instead, the character announces:

"The world knows you're doing something, I think, aren't you?"

Things don't flow here, the pace is uneven, there is no smoothness. The rhythm is bad. Take out "I think," and it still doesn't have the evenness of the earlier phrase.

Rhythm affects not only what the reader sees but what he or she hears. That's right...*hears*! William Zinsser, in his book, *On Writing Well*, puts it succinctly:

Also bear in mind, when you are choosing words and stringing them together, how they sound. This may seem absurd: readers read with their eyes. But actually, they hear what they are reading—in their inner ear—far more than you realize.

See how the following passage affects us in this way. It's from Russell Bank's novel, *Continental Drift*. In the story, a young Haitian woman and her baby son and young nephew are in a frantic escape from Haiti, on a perilous journey towards Florida. The three Haitians are in the hold of an island freighter when the freighter picks up some other Haitians whom the captain orders into the hold. The Haitians want to stay above deck, but the Captain tries to convince them otherwise:

> "Got sumpin down dere better'n up here, mon."
>
> "Yes?"
>
> "Got a gal. Haiti gal down dere, jus' waitin' for a big ol' black Haiti mon to come down an' chat wid her."
>
> "Yes?"
>
> "Haiti gal an' her pickney an' a pretty bwoy down dere wid her."
>
> "Yes? A pretty boy, eh? *Massisi*?
>
> The fat man laughed. "Yas, mon, him a pretty bwoy, all right, but de gal, dat de real beef. Make the journey sweet."
>
> "Yes. So we dry and warm ourself in the morning sun, eh? Then we go chat up the Haiti gal and pretty boy, eh?"
>
> "Eh-eh-eh," the Captain said, laughing, walking aft towards the wheelhouse...

Don't we hear the growing interest in the Haitian, and don't we sense the growing terror in the woman as she hears this conversation? Can't we hear these words, as well as read them?

Why?

First, listen to the dialect. It's almost a singsong cadence. Say the words out loud, speak them. They have a natural tempo, a fluid pace. If the same phrases were stripped of dialect and read as dictionary English, they would lose their flavor—and their rhythm.

Second, note the repetitiveness of "yes?" It sets up a regular beat, a short response after a long phrase, a dum/dum/dum/DUM! This is rhythm because it is so regular and because it follows a pattern.

Third, see how the Captain's speech rhythm differs from the Haitian's. The Captain talks in longer sentences, he *sounds* more expansive. The Haitian speaks in short bursts, as if too many words would make him vulnerable. This contrast in rhythm provides us with another insight: it shows us character, and this, in turn, makes us *hear* not only *what* is said, but *how* it is said.

Writers, sometimes, forget the importance of rhythm in developing the tone of their stories. Good rhythm means a story fits together well; bad rhythm means it is lopsided and uneven. To John Gardner, the late novelist, awareness of rhythm is crucial. Even famous writers, he says:

> ...write with no consciousness of the poetic effects available through prose rhythm. They put wine on the table, put the cigarette in the ashtray, paint the lovers, start the clock ticking, all with no thought of whether the sentences should be fast or slow, light hearted or solemn with wedge-in juxtaposed stresses...

How would we slow down a line of dialogue? Let's take a simple phrase:

> "I'm not sure I want to go."

We can lengthen it and complicate it:

> "The problem certainly is me, and deciding to go is difficult."

Or we can use multisyllable words (note the same number of words as the original, however):

> "I'm undecided whether the effort's worth it."

In either case we have slowed things down, and this, then, says to the reader in the subtlest manner that the tempo and the pace of the story may be changing—at least in this short passage. The writer must know, of course, why he wants the pace to change and what he hopes it will accomplish. But if he's aware of what he's doing, his work will carry his intentions much further.

What if we want to speed things up? What if we want our sentences to move rapidly? Take a look at this passage from Ernest Hemingway's *The Short Happy Life of Francis Macomber*. This is the way the story opens:

It was now lunch time and they were all sitting under the double green fly of the dining tent pretending that nothing had happened.

"Will you have lime juice or lemon squash?" Macomber asked.

"I'll have a gimlet," Robert Wilson told him.

"I'll have a gimlet, too. I need something," Macomber's wife said.

"I suppose it's the thing to do," Macomber agreed. "Tell him to make three gimlets"...

Note the tautness and the tension here. *Something* has happened, and the characters are obviously affected by it. The thing that builds the atmosphere is the staccato-like dialogue, the clipped phrases, the short, quick responses. It is the rhythm of the dialogue that sets the mood and gives added body to what is said. The sentences are short and pointed, and the words are uncomplicated. The characters ask, tell, say and agree...no one *wonders...shudders...shouts...cries...* it is a civilized scene, yet underneath that patina of civility lies a mass of raging emotions. It is this controlled tension that Hemingway's words so well portray, and it is the rhythm of his writing that gives us the mood without his having to spell it out in detail.

The key is something we should remember: Hemingway is *showing* us the drama, not telling us.

William Sloane believed that people have at least two vocabularies and that they switch in and out depending upon to whom they are talking and what they are talking about. What he really means is that our reactions are controlled by the environment within which we find ourselves. "A convict talks one way to his mother," he writes, "another way to his girl or to the warden or to a fellow inmate. A woman tells the same thing differently to a man and to another woman."

Does one talk about the sordid reality of prison life with the same degree of venom no matter who the listener? If it's Mother, don't we say things differently than if it's Cell Mate?

It's a two-step process, really: first, we have to decide what we're going to say; then we have to decide how we're going to say it. We might use almost the same words with both listeners—*I hate this foul place*!...though we might add an adjective with Cell Mate that we wouldn't with Mother.

With Mother, we are looking for sympathy, stroking, nurturing, so our tone of voice would be prodding and plaintive...*I hate this foul place*, he sobbed...

With Cell Mate, we are looking for agreement and approbation...*I hate this miserable foul place*, he spat out...

Different vocabularies, different rhythms...though the same words.

The tone we use would be different; with Cell Mate it would be aggressive, disgusted, certainly mean-sounding; with Mother it would be angry, dispirited, probably seeking help. If we expanded the dialogue, the words with Cell Mate would be short, snappy, harsh, building an atmosphere of blinding fury, and the words with Mother would be lengthier phrases, softer on the ear, slower moving, to give effect to the sense of despondency.

Tempo and pace are what we mean by rhythm. We must be aware of and control these elements to achieve the best dialogue. John Sayles puts it well when he writes:

> ...Rhythm applies to the individual speaker's style and to the pace of the story. People speak in different tempos, breathe more or less in phrasing a sentence, put their sentences together simply or in a more complex way...If you control the rhythm of your dialogue, of your story, you can better hold the reader where you want him, make him want to listen to you.

Part C

Misuse and Abuse of Dialogue

21

Will I Be Sued?

We're in a typewriter trance (or computer catalepsy). Eight hours we've been hitting the keys. There's a whisper of strength left in our brain stem...

We stretch out uncertain fingers.

The last line, the last word, the last syllable, the last letter. Period!

Finished! Our creative soul stares back, phrases and paragraphs and pages shimmering with the good effort.

We've created something and it is ours. No one else has ever written these words and produced these paragraphs in quite the same way.

We own it.

Just as if we'd bought it outright.

It's become property, and it belongs to us. Ask a lawyer, and he or she will say, "people who create works of art have a property right in what they have created. The law recognizes this and supports it."

Having a property right means:

- we can sell what we've created;
- we can license its use;

- we can sue to protect it from being copied;
- we can pass it along to our heirs.

And if what we've created includes dialogue, is that protected too?

The lawyer will have no problem with that. "Dialogue that's created as part of the story is also part of the property. If the creative work is protected, so is the dialogue."

Sounds simple, but of course, it isn't. Sometimes what we create isn't fully protected, even though we may continue to call it our own property. Even though judges and lawyers agree it's our own property.

We're sitting in a movie theatre. It's dark and our attention is fixed on the screen. Suddenly, from the back, there is a shout.

"Fire!"

Then a scream, then another shout.

"Fire!"

Panic erupts, there is pandemonium, people get trampled on their way to the exits.

Later, we find there has been no fire.

"I was trying to create a realistic crowd scene," explains the crestfallen perpetrator. "A work of art."

"No one," glares the somber judge at his sentencing, "no one has the right to cry 'Fire!' in a crowded theatre and claim it to be art. There are limits to everything."

Including "free speech" he might have added.

And including the uses to which we put the property right in our creative work.

The point is: we may own what we create, but the law says we don't have an uncontrolled right to publish it. Writing and publishing don't always go hand-in-hand. What we're going to look at in this chapter are some of the limits our legal system has in place. The "controls" on us as writers.

We start with the general idea that whatever we create, whatever we write—dialogue or narration—has limits. Our legal right to create and publish is *not* unlimited.

An important distinction here. Create *and* publish. Publishing, in the legal sense, means showing it off, letting others see it and read it. Even one other person.

If our creation is never published, never seen, the lawyers can't make a case. Creation, alone, is one thing; publishing is something else.

The "control" is in the publishing.

Now, assuming we decide to publish, various legal limits come into play. The easiest way to understand them is to see them in the negative sense; that is, see what they are designed to prevent. Writers, in other words, are not allowed to write dialogue which:

- could ruin another's reputation (with certain exceptions);
- intrudes on another's private world and discloses facts publicly (with certain exceptions);
- copies other writers' words, phrases, sentences and paragraphs and claims ownership;
- puts words in the mouths of celebrities for commercial purposes, even if they are dead.

It's easy to get the idea that a piece of writing has to negotiate a legal jungle before it can emerge unscathed. Lawyers, perhaps, might have us think this way, but the truth is that writing, like any other form of creative utterance (films, speeches, music, painting, for example) is vigorously protected by the First Amendment to the Constitution, and for the most part the courts are careful to avoid the quagmire of creative warfare. Too much legal intrusion, like too many cooks in the kitchen, can spoil the product. One jurist, Irving R. Kaufman of the Second Circuit Court of Appeals, puts it this way:

...permitting plaintiffs to recover money damages, sometimes very large money damages, from writers and publishers necessarily inhibits creativity. Every case that is brought, even if it does not result in an award, encourages potential defendants to err on the side of caution, thereby depriving society of material that would otherwise have been available...

We know, then, that the lawyerly tail should not wag the creative dog, and that writers have a strong presumption in favor of their own creative efforts. Yet the legal jungle does not disappear just because some judges are more sympathetic than others. Writers can hurt people by what they write, and the law recognizes various forms of redress. Dialogue, in these instances, is a particularly acute weapon, if it's used in a harmful manner. We should remember that as we come to understand what it takes to injure someone else through the words and phrases we use.

Libel

Seventy-five years ago a man by the name of Howard wrote a novel, *God's Man*, in which he depicted adventures in the underworld of New York City. It was a "sensational" book, full of political revelations, bribery, payoffs, cruelties, and other unsavory acts. One chapter he titled "Justice—à la Cornigan," and it concerned the barely civilized conduct of a public magistrate named Cornigan who sat in New York's Jefferson Market Court and dispensed uneven, whimsical, often nasty justice. He was described as "ignorant, brutal, hypocritical, corrupt, shunned by his fellows, bestial of countenance, unjust, dominated by political discussions and grossly unfit. . . ."

Now, it happened that Howard, the author, had once appeared before a real-live New York magistrate named Corrigan, and Howard had come away from that encounter with a bad taste in his mouth.

And after the book appeared, Judge Corrigan also tasted bile. A lawsuit followed.

I'm none of the things he says I am, the real-life judge said. I'm honest and hard working, and I resent being held up to public scorn. . .*and lied about*!

We never knew a judge with almost the same name could be sitting on the same court, said the publisher. An inadvertent error, we're sorry.

Too bad, the court said, but the real-life Judge Corrigan has been libelled by the novel. There's little doubt the character in the book is the same person as the real-life judge. The fact that one letter in the name is different doesn't mean much. Howard, the author, clearly wrote a book "of and concerning" the plaintiff.

And..."Actual malice might be inferred as against the author from the falsity of the publication."

Libel, then, rides on these two tracks: is the person being written about the same or nearly the same person who appears in the novel? Are the things that are written false and therefore malicious?

It wouldn't hurt to gain familiarity with the way judges and lawyers define libel because, after all, it is they who render final judgment on how offensive—or inoffensive—our words will be. Libel, remember, is a form of injury for which damages can be claimed, and the courts try to evaluate such a right to damages against the crucial need to protect and preserve the First Amendment. Every libel case is a balancing between these two forces.

> A publication is libelous on its face when the words impute to the plaintiff the commission of a crime or a contagious disorder tending to exclude him from society, or when the injurious words are spoken or published with respect to his profession or trade, or to disparage him in public office, or tend to bring him into ridicule and contempt...

A judge wrote those words some years ago, but they are still effective today. The law has meandered somewhat, but the essentials remain: *commission of a crime...contagious disorder ...disparage...ridicule and contempt...*

In 1964 the Supreme Court changed things a bit. In the famous case of *New York Times Co. v. Sullivan*, an advertisement criticized opponents of the civil-rights struggle, particularly those in Montgomery, Alabama. The Chief of Police (who wasn't mentioned by name in the advertisement) took issue with this and claimed he had been libelled. The Supreme Court said that the Chief was a public person, and therefore, to win on libel, he had to show the newspaper had "actual" malice towards him—lies and misstatements that were directed precisely at him. The fact that his reputation was damaged (even though he wasn't named in the advertisement) isn't enough without showing other things.

There must be some form of malice—at least in so far as public persons are concerned—to prove libel, and the more we tell unsavory lies about another, the more malicious the courts will find what we write.

With private persons the standard is different: so long as what is published is false and defamatory and is "of and concerning" the person who is doing the complaining, libel can be claimed.

But let's stick with malice for a moment. It's a deep-seated dislike, often with an urge to see someone else suffer and suffer severely. It is hard-hearted, revenge-seeking words and phrases that go far beyond simple falsehoods, and in a legal context they must be untrue. And if the courts find malice—it doesn't matter whether the subject is a public or private person—that person has been libelled.

A few years ago, Gwen Davis Mitchell published a steamy novel called *Touching*. In it there was a scene at a nude encounter session between the therapist in charge of the procedure and a minister whose wife had been reluctant to join in. The author had actually attended such a session, and before being allowed to come had signed an agreement not to write about what she saw and heard. Nevertheless, two months later she began her book, and when the psychologist in charge of the therapy session saw it, he sued, claiming a nude encounter session in the book was a malicious replay of one of his sessions; that it was false, defamatory and held him up to ridicule and contempt.

Not so, said the author. The therapist in my book is a "fat Santa Claus type with long white hair, white sideburns, a cherubic rosy face and rosy forearms." You, Dr. Plaintiff, are clean shaven with short hair.

It's still me, insisted the plaintiff. You violated our agreement, and you have defamed me. Compare your dialogue with what went on at the session you attended.

The court did, and here's the crucial similarity:

Book Excerpt	Actual Session Transcript

The minister was telling us how the experience had gotten him further back to God.

And all the time he was getting closer to God, he was being moved further away from his wife, who didn't understand, she didn't understand at all. She didn't realize what was coming out of the sensitivity training sessions he was conducting in the church.

(H)e felt, he more than felt, he knew, that if she didn't begin coming to the nude marathons and try to grasp what it was all about, the marriage would be over.

"You better bring her to the next marathon," Simon said.

"I've been trying," said the minister. "I only pray she comes."

"You better do better than pray," said Simon. "You better grab her by the c_____ and drag her here."

"I can only try."

"You can do more than try,

"I've come a little way."

"I'd like to know about your wife. She hasn't been to a marathon?"

"No."

"Isn't she interested? Has no need?"

"I don't—she did finally say she would like to go to a standard sensitivity training session somewhere. She would be—I can't imagine her in a marathon. She can't imagine it."

"Why?"

"Neither could I when I first came."

"Yeh. She might. I don't know."

"It certainly would be a good idea for two reasons: one, the minor one is that you are involved here, and if she were in the same thing, and you could come to some of the couple ones, it would be helpful to you. But more than that, almost a definite recipe for breaking up a marriage is

Book Excerpt

Actual Session Transcript

Alex. You can grab her by the c_____."

"A man with that kind of power, whether it comes from God or from his own manly strength he doesn't know he has, can drag his wife here by the f_____ c_____."

"I know," Alex said softly, "I know."

for one person to go into growth groups and sense change and grow. . ."

"I know that."

"Boy they sure don't want that, and once they're clear they don't need that mate anymore, and they are not very patient."

"But it is true, the more I get open the more walls are built between us. And it's becoming a fairly intelligent place, a fairly open place, doing moderate sensitivity eyeballing stuff with the kids. I use some of these techniques teaching our class work."

Both passages deal with the general subject of enticing the man's wife to attend a nude encounter session. Both discuss the fact that when only one member of a couple experiences the effects of nude encounter, the marriage itself is in jeopardy. And both touch on how reluctant the wife is to come.

But note the different tone of the dialogue in each passage. In the book excerpt the therapist is foul-mouthed, threatening, overbearing and utterly male chauvinistic. In the actual transcript session, the therapist is tempered, reasoned, concerned. He's interested in his subject without trying to bully him in any way.

Can dialogue be libellous?

Here's the court:

Mitchell's reckless disregard for the truth was apparent

from her knowledge of the truth of what transpired at the encounter, and the literary portrayals of that encounter. Since she attended sessions, there can be no suggestion that she did not know the true facts...

Actual malice, said the court, a "reckless disregard for the truth." Mitchell knew the real-life therapist didn't use foul language during a therapy session and didn't conduct his session the way Simon Herford did. She provided a false portrayal, and she did so with full knowledge of what the truth was.

Dialogue libel is the result. Actual malice is the reason.

Generally, the tip-off inquiry in any libel matter is whether the published material is "of and concerning" the person who is doing the complaining. That is, can a particular person be identified and does the writing affect the reputation and standing of that person in the community?

Obviously, if either of these questions can be answered "no," there has been no libel.

But to decide whether anything has been "of and concerning" someone, there are certain steps we can follow.

- *Is the work presented as fiction?* If it is, then the chances are reduced there could be libel exposure because fiction, by its very nature, is of the imagination.

- *How closely does the character in the book resemble the character who is complaining?* Obviously, the tighter the resemblance, the more danger there is. Among other things, we can look at the ages, physical appearances, and names of the characters for any similarities, and we can see how parallel the location of the action is and whether there is a close identity of occupation.

- *Are there similarities between events in the book and events in the life of the person complaining?* The closer the similarities are, of course, the more vulnerable we make ourselves.

- *How big a role does the character play in the book?* The more important the character, the more extensive the information to establish "of and concerning."

Some years ago, a well-conceived novel was published, detailing events leading up to and during a trial for murder on Michigan's Upper Peninsula. *Anatomy of a Murder* was the story of a man who killed another because the victim had raped the killer's wife. As it happened, this paralleled a real-life murder and trial in the same geographic location, and the widow of the rapist claimed she had been libelled in the book.

The key is how she was portrayed. "Janice Quill" was described as "that dame with the dyed red hair and livid scar on her right cheek who had sworn at him in everything but Arabian... who'd ever forget such a noisy foul-mouthed harridan?"

You have me using foul language and doing other disreputable things, Hazel Wheeler, the real-life widow, claimed. I'm not that kind of person.

Precisely the point, said the publisher. How can it be you when your own words deny the likeness? The portrayal is certainly not "of and concerning" you.

It's me, all right, continued the widow, even if you have me acting like a different person. You describe me with dyed red hair and a scar on the cheek... well, during the trial I used a henna rinse on my hair, and my face showed I had been recently scratched.

Sorry, said the court. "In our opinion, any reasonable person who read the book and was in a position to identify Hazel Wheeler with Janice Quill would more likely conclude that the author created the latter in an ugly way so that no one would identify her with Hazel Wheeler."

The portrayal is not "of and concerning" anyone. It is fiction.

And treating it as fiction makes a big difference. Where is the libel if the characters are fictional? Who has been injured, what has been the damage?

So, the person doing the complaining has to show that the author meant to describe him or her with the offensive words, phrases and dialogue. It may be called a novel, the complainer will say, but it's acutally directed at me, it's really not fiction.

Let's look at the similarities, the court will say.

And the closer the similarities come, the more chance there could be libel. Unless it's clear that a fictional work was intended.

Take the notorious Son-of-Sam killings in New York during the 1970s. Clearly, these were real-live events, but Jimmy Breslin and Dick Schaap wrote a novel, .44, about the crimes, the police investigation to solve them, and the ultimate disposition of the case. There was no attempt to make this into a "docudrama" or to portray it as any other form of nonfiction. It was fiction, and the book so stated. However, one passage caught the critical eye of a sheriff in upstate New York. The passage describes a conversation between Carillo, an inspector on the New York police force, and two of his men, Swanson and Seibert. They have been working their way through a computer print-out of all registered owners of .44-caliber Bulldog revolvers in the New York, New Jersey, Connecticut, and Pennsylvania areas.

"We been up to our asses in this thing," Seibert said. He had received the communication and was attempting to answer it. "See Inspector? We got a guy here in Malone, New York. We ask the Sheriff up there to go to the guy and have him fire his weapon and send us the slug so we can test it, and you know what the Sheriff in Malone says? He says, 'I got no way to do that.' We tell him, 'just get a pipe and shoot down the pipe into a tub of water.' The Sheriff says to me, 'Send me a pipe'."

"What did you do with the guy?" Carillo asked.

"Nothing, Inspector," Seibert said. "That's what we're sitting here talking about."

A hand began to scour Carillo's insides with sandpaper.

"This is tough going, Inspector," Swanson said. "Maybe here and there only we get a break. Like this one here in Hamden, up in Connecticut. Guy died. So we can go past him now. Otherwise, we'd have to stop at the name and go all through what we're going through with this quiff in Malone.''

The Sheriff, whose name was Lyons, was not pleased with the dialogue between the police officers. He found it offensive and defamatory.

He was, after all, the Sheriff in Malone, New York.

You accuse me of incompetence, he claimed, and you call me names. 'Quiff'' is a well-known slang phrase for a sexual pervert. Your accusations are false, and I demand damages.

You weren't even involved in the Son-of-Sam investigation, the publisher retorted. How can this be "of and concerning" you?

There's only one Sheriff in Malone, New York, and that's me, said Lyons.

Not enough, said the court. "The work clearly states that it is fiction and that, combined with plaintiff's admission that he did not participate in the Son-of-Sam investigation, requires the conclusion that the passage is not actionable.''

Sheriff Lyons has no claim.

But note carefully that the offending language was the dialogue. And note, too, that if Lyons had been part of the investigation, the decision might have gone the other way. The things that Lyons complained about were enough to hold him up to ridicule and contempt within his locality, *provided* it could be shown the character described in the book actually was he, that the descriptions and criticisms were "of and concerning" him.

Libel must be considered against a background of the author's intention. If the facts show there was malice in the offensive portrayal (a reckless disregard of the truth), and that it was false and that the similarities between the person doing the complaining and the character in the book are substantial, we're going to have a problem.

And doing it in dialogue doesn't make the problem any easier. So . . .

- clearly label all fictional material;
- avoid a disreputable portrayal of a character known to be alive (unless it's a truthful portrayal);
- avoid a disreputable portrayal of a fictional character who closely resembles a known living person (unless it's a truthful portrayal);
- when we put words in a fictional character's mouth, make sure we understand whom they might offend, why and where.

Right to Privacy

Morris Polokoff was an elderly lawyer, living out the fruits of a successful law practice. One day he was surprised to discover he had made the pages of a novel, *The Algonquin Project*. It was the story of two young aides to General Eisenhower during the Second World War and their planned assassination of a military man modelled after George Patton. They needed only an assassin, and they sought the "good offices" of imprisoned hoodlum Lucky Luciano for that purpose. The book described a visit to Luciano at the prison by Polokoff, in company with two members of the OSS (forerunner of the CIA), and their request for help. Polokoff, many years before the book came out, had helped represent Luciano in a compulsory prostitution charge (in which there was a conviction) and then handled certain work relating to the appeal. During the war, Polokoff had also assisted U.S. Naval Intelligence by acting as an information conduit between them and Luciano and going to see Luciano in prison a number of times.

I've been libelled! shouted Polokoff. The things you have me do in the book never happened. It's false and defamatory.

It's a novel, a work of fiction, stated the publisher. We're not claiming you actually did those things.

It's "of and concerning" me—you even use my right name! What could be clearer?

Sorry, said the court. Even though the book "parallels" Polokoff's wartime experiences, a reader of average intelligence would not conclude that the author intended people to believe Polokoff actually tried to procure an assassin. No libel.

Maybe it's not libel, Polokoff acknowledged, but you have certainly invaded my right to privacy.

How can that be? the publisher argued. This is a work of fiction; everyone knows it's not a true story.

You have interferred with my right to be let alone, Polokoff argued. It doesn't matter whether the book is fiction, you used my real name and you "paralleled" my wartime experiences. No one has a right to do that without my permission.

We agree, said the court. Polokoff wins.

The right to privacy is just this: the right to be let alone, to be free from unwarranted intrusion. As writers, we must understand these limitations on what we write about and whom we write about.

Our right to privacy is different from our right to be free from libel. Privacy is not based on damages to our reputation, as is libel, nor is it based on the truth or falsity of what is written. Privacy is simply our right to have nothing written about our private affairs—good or bad—or to have ourselves portrayed— good or bad—without our permission.

The general feeling is that our privacy is invaded when one or more of the following things occurs:

- our physical solitude has been disrupted;
- aspects of our private life have been publicly disclosed;
- there has been publicity which has placed us in a false light;
- our name or likeness has been appropriated and used for someone else's commercial benefit.

Dialogue can be a privacy invader just as any form of narrative can. Our own private words can be published. . .or we can be portrayed and words put into our mouths. . .or we can be named and described, even debated about. . .the important thing to remember is that whatever dialogue is used, it is our *right to be let alone* that we can protect.

Our privacy right—insofar as it is protected in court—is only about a hundred years old. The English common law never paid much attention to it. But in 1890 an article in the *Harvard Law Review* by Louis D. Brandeis and Samuel D. Warren proposed the need for some legally protected right to privacy because of the proliferation of gossip that had found its way into newspapers, often garnished by photographs. Gossip had become a business, they argued, and there need to be limits:

> The intensity and complexity of life, attendant upon advancing civilization, have rendered necessary some retreat from the world, and man, under the refining influence of culture, has become more sensitive to publicity, so that solitude and privacy have become more essential to the individual. . .

Many states jumped on the idea and within a short period a right to privacy became established legal doctrine. Newsworthy items, of course, were exceptions, as were most subjects of biographies and autobiographies. But that left a large area of uncertainty, and the courts became the place to settle things.

Zelma Cason was an earthy, strong-willed Florida woman who had been appointed a census-taker in 1930. In those days Florida had large rural pockets, and the census-taker travelled the bush on horseback. Margorie Kinnan Rawlings decided to accompany Zelma on her census-taking, and the result was a book, *Cross-Creek*, which was highly praised. In the book, Rawlings refers to "Zelma" and describes her as "an ageless spinster":

> "I cannot decide whether she should have been a man or a mother. She combines the more violent characteristics of both, and those who ask for or accept her manifold ministrations think nothing of being cursed loudly at the very instant of being tenderly fed, clothed, nursed or guided through their troubles. . ."

Zelma was bothered by this narrative description, but then Rawlings went further; she used dialogue, she gave us the words out of Zelma's mouth:

"It's a _____ blessing for us not many Yankees have seen country like this, or they'd move in on us worse than Sherman," Zelma said.

Zelma said, "I forgot that woman was buried back here."

My profane friend Zelma, the census-taker, said "The b_____s killed the egrets for their plummage until the egrets gave out. They killed alligators for their hides until the alligators gave out. If the frogs ever give out, the sons of _____s will starve to death."

"Well," Zelma said, "a Mediterranean fruit fly'd be a fool to lay an egg tonight."

You make me sound awful, Zelma complained, you've taken my private words and put them out for all to see.

It's a loving portrayal, Rawlings argued, I'm not trying to hold you up to ridicule. Anyway, at no time in the book do I use your last name. No one has to know it was you.

That doesn't matter, Zelma insisted. You and I know those are my private words, said privately. You have no right to publish them without my permission.

The court agreed and disagreed with both Zelma and Rawlings. The book "portrays the plaintiff as a fine and attractive personality, [but] it is nevertheless a rather vivid and intimate character sketch."

- No harm to Zelma's reputation, *but...*
- An invasion of her privacy, *even though...*
- she may have suffered no financial damages.

The point needs repeating: be careful whose words we use and when we use them; if they are intimate words, if they are said privately, if the speaker's identity is known, privacy has been invaded.

And we'll have some explaining to do.

Dialogue remains a prime privacy invader, and we need look no further than a purported biography of a Hall of Fame baseball pitcher, Warren Spahn, a few years back. The author never interviewed his subject and relied on newspaper and magazine copy for most of his information. Even so, the story is dramatized to the point of manufactured dialogue. Here's a conversation between Spahn and his father's doctor concerning the psychological effects of an injury to Spahn's elbow:

"This—well—breakdown let's call it - might have happened at any time, for any number of similar reasons. No, Warren, it would be morally wrong, in my opinion, to fix the blame for your father's illness on your misfortune."

Warren nodded grimly. "What you're trying to tell me is it's not my fault that it's my fault, isn't that right, Doctor? That my getting hurt was kind of the straw that broke Pop's back?"...

Here's another example, a conversation between Spahn and his fiancée at his surprise return from Europe:

Then, in Tulsa one evening, Lorene Southard was just sitting down to dinner when the door-bell rang. "Now who can that be?" she said aloud to herself. She strode briskly across the room and opened the door. A startled cry escaped her lips.

"Warren!" she gasped.

"Surprise!" Spahn cried. He swept Lorene off her feet and carried her into the room. "Surprise! Surprise!" he kept shouting as he swung her around in his arms.

"Warren! Warren!" she laughed and cried at the same time. "Put me down!"

This is an invasion of privacy, Spahn argued. The author even has the facts wrong. When I returned from Europe, I telephoned Lorene *first* and then she met me at the train station and we went off to dinner.

I'm entitled to use literary license, the author insisted. Everyone knows a book like this doesn't have to be word-for-word accurate. Anyway, what are you complaining about? The book praises you. Dramatic license is my right, especially since you are a public figure.

You've made me say and do things that weren't true, Spahn shot back. You are holding me up to false light, and that's a violation of my right to privacy, even if I'm patted on the back.

The court agreed. Even though Spahn is a public figure and must therefore suffer some public comment and scrutiny, this is simply too much. Everyone, even public figures, has the right to be free from certain basic commercial exploitation of name and personality. The manufactured dialogue and shoddy research efforts showed the broad license the author intended to take. An invasion of privacy, absolutely!

For writers the key is this: beware of manufactured dialogue, especially when it puts the subject in a *false light* (has him or her saying and doing things he/she did not say or do, so that a false impression is created). Otherwise, we are trifling with the subject's right to be let alone.

The general run of privacy cases has also spawned an offshoot we call the "right of *publicity*." This is the right of celebrities to prevent their persona from being used for commercial purposes without consent. The privacy aspect of it is that each of us has the right to control those portions of our persona (name, likeness, etc.) we wish to control, and when we are celebrities, we have the right to control publicity others may generate from our persona.

It is the private *we*!

And the interesting thing is that this right of publicity runs beyond our own deaths. The general right of privacy such as the one Zelma Cason pursued against Marjorie Kinnan Rawlings stops at death. But with the right of publicity it can go on and on:

- Clyde Beatty's heirs sued to stop the use of his name in connection with circuses, even though he had been dead some years.
- Elvis Presley's estate has been vigorous in preventing the use of his name in connection with commercial products almost from the moment he died.

Dialogue fits in here, too. Suppose we take a deceased celebrity and put words in his or her mouth and utilize his or her likeness for commercial purposes, such as the promotion of certain products, or revelation of heretofore unknown facts. We could have a problem. We use dialogue to make our point, and we must be careful.

Remember Agatha Christie? Way back in 1923, as a young bride, she disappeared for eleven days while she was married to Sir Archibald Christie. Throughout her life she never divulged where she had gone or whom she had seen, even though the disappearance had been widely publicized. Shortly after her death, a book, *Agatha*, was published, and it set out to recreate what had happened to her during that time. The book portrayed her as unstable and engaged in a sinister plot to murder her husband's mistress and then regain his love. The author never indicated whether this scenario was true, but simply let the book stand for itself (though it was called a "novel" on the dust jacket). Words, of course, were put in Agatha Christie's mouth, and the book's purpose was to exploit her name, reputation, and an enduring mystery in her own life.

We control who will publicize Agatha's name and persona, said her estate, and they sued, claiming a violation of the right of publicity.

Everyone knows this is a fictionalized treatment, answered the publisher. No one would believe it actually happened.

The estate wasn't convinced. You use Agatha's name, you are exploiting it to sell your books, they insisted.

Not so, retorted the publisher. We are speculating on an event no one knows the truth about. It is simple dramatic license.

Correct, said the court. "The only facts contained in the book appear to be the names of Mrs. Christie, her husband, her daughter, and Mr. Neeley; and that Mrs. Christie disappeared for eleven days. The remainder is mainly conjecture, surmise and fiction..."

No right of publicity.

But the court made clear that the peculiar facts of this case shouldn't be overdone. The key is whether or not the average reader would believe that what was depicted actually happened. If the reader could be led in this direction, then Agatha Christie's estate would have a strong claim for a violation of her right of publicity even though she was long gone.

Mark the court's words:

> ...the right of publicity does not attach here, where a fictionalized account of an event in the life of a public figure is depicted in a novel or movie it is evident to the public that the events so depicted are fictitious...

But if the events are portrayed as having taken place, even though the subject is dead, and dialogue is part of the mix?

We could be in for a long day in court.

Unless we make sure that what we write is fiction and everyone knows it's fiction.

Dialogue we create must be judged on the same legal basis as any other aspect of fiction writing. It can be harmful, if another can demonstrate the dialogue was directed at him or her and the effects have caused injury to a reputation; it's also harmful where matters are divulged about an individual and no over-riding public interest is at stake. Dialogue is a powerful tool, and while there are pitfalls, it's more important to remember that the courts find little joy in limiting our rights to free expression. What we produce as dialogue is the essence of creativity, and how it has worked itself out on the written page is part of a process that mystifies as much as it enlightens:

> ...And so it is that the work of a writer reflects the parts that he has collected throughout his life. Events and characters may be refined and modified so that even the

author would not recognize them as resulting from real life. Nevertheless, real-life experiences are the source of all artistic inspiration. . .*

"See!" says the author, "my life is my treasure."

"And," adds the reader, "dialogue is why it sparkles!"

---

* "Real People and Fiction" by Dan Rosen and Charles L. Babcock, 7 *Hastings Journal of Communication and Entertainment Law* 221, Winter, 1985.

Bibliography

Books

Allott, Miriam. *Novelists on the Novel*. New York: Columbia University Press, 1959.

Barasch, Marc, and Martin, Russell, eds. *Writers of the Purple Sage*. New York: Viking, 1984.

Bocca, Geoffrey. *You Can Write a Novel*. Englewood Cliffs, N.J.: Prentice-Hall, 1983.

Cassill, R.V. *Writing Fiction*. Englewood Cliffs, N.J.: Prentice-Hall, 1975.

Cawelti, John G. *Adventure, Mystery and Romance: Formula Stories As Art and Popular Culture*. Chicago: University of Chicago Press, 1976.

Clark, Glenn. *A Manual of the Short Story Art*. New York: Macmillan Co., 1923.

Crawford, Tad. *The Writer's Legal Guide*. New York: Hawthorn Books Inc., 1977.

Curry, Peggy Simson. *Creating Fiction From Experience*. Boston: The Writer Inc., 1964.

Fox, Edward S. *How to Write Stories That Sell*. Boston: The Writer Inc., 1961.

Gardner, John. *The Art of Fiction*. New York: Alfred A. Knopf, 1984.

Grabo, Carl H. *The Art of the Short Story*. New York: Charles Scribner's Sons, 1913.

Grabo, Carl H. *The Technique of the Novel*. New York: Charles Scribner's Sons, 1964.

Highsmith, Patricia. *Plotting and Writing Suspense Fiction*. Boston: The Writer Inc., 1972.

Humphrey, Robert. *Stream of Consciousness In the Modern Novel*. Berkeley: University of California Press, 1955.

Kawin, Bruce. *The Mind of the Novel*. Princeton: Princeton University Press, 1982.

Madden, David. *A Primer of the Novel For Readers and Writers*. Metuchen, N.J.: Scarecrow Press Inc., 1980.

Malin, Irving, ed. *Truman Capote's In Cold Blood: A Critical Handbook*. Belmont, Calif.: Wadsworth Publishing Co., 1968.

May, Charles E., ed. *Short Story Theories*. Athens, Ohio: Ohio University Press, 1969.

Noble, June and William. *Steal This Plot*. Middlebury, Vt.: Paul S. Eriksson, 1985.

Sloane, William. *The Craft of Writing*. Julia Sloane, ed. New York: W.W. Norton and Co., 1979.

Stevick, Philip, ed. *The Theory of the Novel*. New York: Free Press, 1967.

Summerlian, Leon. *Techniques of Fiction Writing*. New York: Doubleday and Co., 1968.

Vivante, Arturo. *Writing Fiction*. Boston: The Writer Inc., 1980.

White, E.B. and K.S., eds. *A Subtreasury of American Humor*. New York: Random House, 1941.

Williams, Blanche Colton. *A Handbook on Short Story Writing*. New York: Dodd Mead, 1920.

Wittenburg, Philip. *The Protection of Literary Property*. Boston: The Writer Inc., 1958.

Zinsser, William. *On Writing Well*. New York: Harper & Row, 1976.

Zweig, Paul. *The Adventurer*. New York: Basic Books, 1974.

Articles

Alpern, Lynn, and Blumenfield, Esther. "Writing Humor—But Seriously, Folks." *Writer's Digest*, January, 1982.

Block, Lawrence. "A Stitch In Time." *Writer's Digest*, June, 1983.

—"The Shadow Knows." *Writer's Digest*, July, 1981.

—"He Said She Said." *Writer's Digest*, February, 1977.

Blythe, Hal, and Sweet, Charlie. "Taking Care of Business." *Writer's Digest*, February, 1987.

Burgess, Anthony. "What Is Pornography?" In *Perspectives on Pornography*, edited by Douglas A. Hughes. New York: St. Martin's Press, 1970.

Carr, Robyn. " 'Dialogue,' Said the Writer, 'Is a Fantastic Tool For Enriching and Enlivening Your Fiction'." *Writer's Digest*, February, 1984.

Edwards, Margaret. "From Movies to 'Talkies'." *The Writer*, November, 1976.

Estleman, Loren D. "Five Ways to Strengthen Fiction With Dialogue. *Writer's Digest*, March, 1983.

Franco, Marjorie. "Dialogue With a Purpose." *The Writer*, April, 1980.

Gerson, Noel B. "Making Dialogue Speak For You." *The Writer*, July, 1979.

Huttner, Richard. "Stop Look and Listen." *The Writer*, January, 1980.

Reece, Colleen L. "Simon Retorts...Exclaims...States...Simon Says." *Writer's Digest*, January, 1984.

Sayles, John. "Writing Dialogue." *The Writer*, January, 1978.

Sheldon, Sidney. "The Professional Response." *The Writer*, June, 1984.

Sullivan, Eleanor. "A Few Tips For Mystery Writers." *Writer's Digest*, April, 1987.

Index